Christmas

with
Southern Living
1982

Compiled & Edited by Jo Voce and Candace N. Conard

Oxmoor House, Inc. Birmingham

Copyright© 1982 by Oxmoor House, Inc.
Book Division of Southern Progress Corporation
P.O. Box 2463, Birmingham, Alabama 35201

Library of Congress Number: 81-80138

ISBN: 0-8487-0535-1
Manufactured in the United States of America
First Printing

Contents

Introduction

Christmas with Southern Living 1982 celebrates a season of joy and good will. Christmas is our most traditional holiday when we remember and treasure all the Christmases that have come before, and it is also our most creative season as we make new gifts and decorations and add a new recipe to a holiday menu that has been honored for years. Christmas is, too, a family time. Santa, the tree, the stockings, Christmas dinner—all the best efforts of Christmas are directed toward a family celebration. Southerners, those lovers of tradition and family gatherings, naturally find Christmas the most joyful of seasons. *Christmas with Southern Living 1982* is designed to help with all the preparations for the holiday.

Christmas Around the South presents a cornucopia of pageants and decorations from all around the region. Decorating for the Holidays offers new projects and arrangements for you to make and add to your collection of favorite Christmas adornments. Choose a whole theme or a single ornament. A Christmas Bazaar of ideas is overflowing with gifts and decorations, so many that it will be hard to decide where to begin. Celebrations from the Kitchen serves up scrumptious recipes for tasty additions to your traditional Christmas meal. Kids in the Kitchen is devoted to children's favorites: taffy to pull, mints to shape, lollipops to coat with sugar. Selections from Party & Gift Ideas will help with entertaining and provide a gift that is always appropriate and warmly appreciated. The Joys of Giving suggests a variety of decorations and gifts for easy shopping, and a Christmas Journal will help to organize all the activities.

With this abundance of projects and ideas come our best wishes for a joyous Christmas.

Christmas around the South

One of the joys of Christmas is that it inspires us to share in creative projects as neighbors work together to make dramatic decorations and to stage pageants. In this chapter, we have recorded some of the many joyful and exuberant expressions of the season that can be found all around the South.

Christmas trees come in many forms, but we are still surprised by a giant cactus bedecked with lights. The lights of McAdenville, North Carolina, impress us simply because there are so *many* of them. A truck loaded with trees reminds us that all our Christmas trees begin similarly but become individual expressions when we decorate them.

Traditions and historical events are reflected in numerous festivities around the South. In San Antonio, the various pageants reflect the flavor of their Spanish ancestry. In St. Augustine, the Grand Christmas Illumination is based on a period of English rule. And in Colonial Williamsburg, the Christmas decorations, events, and games re-create those of the colonial period of Virginia's history. Some celebrations have become identified with particular cities. Baltimore firemen continue the tradition of a Christmas Garden, and in Fort Worth, Texas, the whole city lights up for the season.

We hope that you will enjoy seeing how Christmas is kept across the South and that you will write and share with us the expressions of Christmas joy that you find in your own neighborhood.

The Christmas Garden of Engine House No. 45 in Baltimore, Maryland. *A Christmas garden is a display of miniature scenes under a Christmas tree and a phenomenon of Baltimore. Beyond this general statement, a definition becomes impossible, because the displays are so varied that they defy labels. Then, too, there is no order in the display; a New York skyscraper and a balloon over the Swiss Alps may be side by side in the display, their only common link the pleasure they bring to the builder. Gardens defy reasons; they are built for the fun of it and they are displayed for the fun of it.*

The passion for garden building reached its height in the 1940s and 1950s. Numerous gardens were constructed, many of them quite elaborate.

The firehouses of Baltimore, however, had the most impressive gardens. Almost every station built a garden, and visitors would stand in lines to view the marvelous handiwork. Gradually, however, the firehouses stopped setting up the gardens. All the firehouses, that is, except one.

Engine House No. 45 in northwest Baltimore keeps the tradition alive by maintaining an extensive garden—12 feet by 40 feet, to be precise. Last year, approximately 23,000 people visited the garden. This year, for the twenty-ninth year, it will be in place from mid-December until about January 10.

The firemen begin preparing their garden in early September, assembling their impressive display between runs. Each year, the garden is built anew, and the garden is different from year to year. Some buildings and trains are purchased through the only source of funds, the donations of visitors. Beyond the few purchases, the sources depend upon creative "finding." A developer's model of downtown Baltimore may be combined with scrap-heap materials. There may be a baseball diamond, a skating rink, a coal-mining operation. Some of the scenes have working parts. In the skating rink shown here, for example, a tiny motor turns the rink so that the figures "skate."

The firefighters let their imaginations take them to many places—and then they build those imaginary lands in miniature. It is impossible to say whether the garden brings more pleasure to the firefighters or to the many people who visit the display.

San Antonio's Christmas Festivals. *Christmas in San Antonio is celebrated with the flair of a Mexican fiesta as the city fills its holiday with the joy and pageantry of its heritage and customs. One of the liveliest events is the Fiesta Navideña. Market Square—with all its wares and shoppers—becomes even more colorful with the addition of dancers and musicians. The city's Ballet Folklorico (shown at left) swirls to the Latin music in costumes as gay and colorful as the sound. Nearby, children wait in lines with their pets for the blessing of the animals.*

In the evening, the River Walk sparkles with the colored lights that decorate the trees, with the softer glow of luminaries along the edge of the Walk, and with candles carried by a procession of participants in the ritual of Las Posados. Searching for "room at the inn," the carolers make their way past many inns to arrive at the last stop, the manger. The end of the search is marked by a celebration with refreshments and a piñata party.

Other celebrations in the city include the performance of Los Pastores, a miracle play brought to the area 2½ centuries ago by conquistadors and missionaries, and a mariachi mass (shown above) in which trumpets, violins, and guitars fill the old adobe walls of the Mission San José.

Saguaro in Paradise Valley. *This stately saguaro stands sentry against the winter sky. When it is bedecked with colored lights, we recognize it immediately as—of course—a Christmas tree that is available only to those in the Southwest.*

Christmas in Colonial Williamsburg. *An impromptu gathering of carolers (far left) adds gaity and spontaneity to the holiday schedule, and spicy gingerbread men have all the dignity and charm of those formed 200 years ago in the same antique walnut cookie mold. In Colonial Williamsburg, Christmas is kept as it was two centuries ago. Visitors can walk through this living museum and look into the daily lives of the people who lived in the Royal Colony of Virginia.*

The Christmas season officially opens in mid-December with the ceremonial lighting of candles, the booming of artillery and muskets, a variety of entertainment, and a grand flourish of fireworks—all authentic forms of celebration in the colonial period. Throughout the Christmas season, celebrations of the holiday extend from the elegant Governor's Palace to the simplest shop. Authentic—and timeless—decorations of garlands and greens are on almost every door, and visitors who want to do more than just look can attend special classes where they learn to make many of the arrangements. In the restaurants, Southern delicacies are served by costumed butlers and waiters. There are bonfires and carolers, a romantic comedy and dancing, a family celebration and a firing demonstration by a garrison regiment. The visitor can watch tradesmen and craftsmen in authentic costume and authentic shops as they carry on the trade of the community. Popular colonial games include a cherry pie-eating contest, pitching quoits, greased pole climb, and hoop rolling. Each visitor takes home with him a bit of the spirit of Christmas celebrations from the past.

Appalachian Santa. *Deep in the mountains of Appalachia, Santa, an unusual vision on horseback, rides through the snow-covered hills to deliver gifts.*

Beech Mountain at Banner Elk, North Carolina.
A ski resort is a favorite holiday vacation spot. At Beech Mountain, the highest ski area in the southeast, four ski lifts glide skiers to slopes that are graded for all levels, beginner to expert.

The luminaries of El Paso. *A luminary is lit by the soft and gentle glow of a candle, but in El Paso, Texas, this glow is multiplied a thousand-fold by the many luminaries sprinkled throughout the city.*

On Christmas Eve, Pennsylvania Circle is transformed from a quiet suburban neighborhood to a glowing wonderland by the soft radiance of the luminaries that outline the streets and sidewalks of the circle. And when the Junior League held its Christmas Fair, luminaries were arranged on a large wooden platform to become a tree.

A luminary is made by cuffing the top of a paper bag, adding a base of sand inside the bag, and setting a candle into the sand. These simple lights are a tradition in the Southwest, used to mark the eves of saints' days and especially the observance of Christmas Eve. They are said to be symbolic of the fires of the shepherds who watched their flocks in the fields near Bethlehem.

St. Augustine's Grand Christmas Illumination. *A British garrison comes to life again as St. Augustine, Florida, celebrates with pomp and ceremony based on two decades of British rule (1763-1784). English law dictated that the city gates be locked at sunset, and residents were required to carry candles or other lights for easy identification.*

Today, in St. Augustine, Christmas is celebrated by participants wearing authentic 18th-century dress. A crowd gathers in the plaza in front of Government

House. A church bell chimes the hour, the rules are read, and the command is given to "Light your lights." Candles, torches, and homemade lanterns appear in the crowd, and a Fife and Drum Corps strikes the pace. Led by units of costumed "Redcoats," the procession winds through the narrow streets of Old St. Augustine and back again. Along the way, the procession swells as it is joined by up to a thousand townspeople and tourists—many in costume.

When the procession again reaches Government House, the soldiers, using oldtime muskets, fire a "volley of joy" in honor of the special holiday, and the musicians break into "God Save the King." Cheers and drum rolls signal the end of the ceremony, and participants re-enter the present as candles and torches give way to brighter lights.

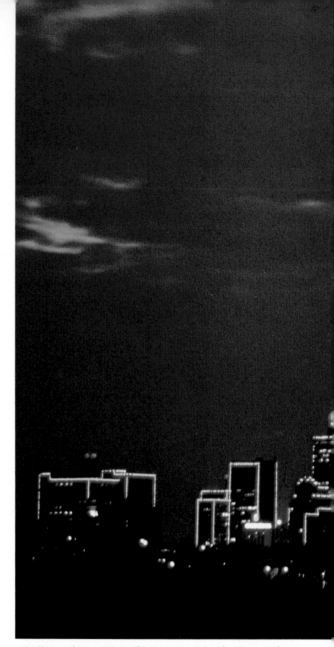

Skyline of Fort Worth. *In Fort Worth, Texas, the entire city lights up for Christmas. The tradition of lighting the skyline began in 1959 when only one building was outlined against the winter night. The following year, a local association urged other building owners to follow suit, and the cooperative effort began. By 1981, more than fifty firms throughout the city were lighting their buildings. The lights are traditionally turned on simultaneously the day after Thanksgiving, and they burn from 5:30 p.m. until midnight each night until January 1.*

Christmas trees en route. *This truck is making its misty way along Interstate 40—that long, long highway that crosses the country from North Carolina to California and replaces the old Route 66. Soon these trees will be decorated with the twinkle and glitter of lights and ornaments, and the magic of Christmas will begin anew.*

11

The Christmas Trees of McAdenville, North Carolina. *In this town of fewer than 1000 residents, there are so many Christmas trees that McAdenville, NC, has been called Christmastown, USA, and tourists come by the thousands to walk or drive along the streets.*

The decorations began in 1957 when the Men's Club decided to decorate just the center of town. The next year, a few wreaths were added. Then the management of Pharr Yarns/Stowe Mills offered to furnish trees and electricity for a more elaborate display. Now, live cedar trees planted in each yard have grown to be quite tall. Members of the volunteer fire department start as early as September to check the lights and decorate the trees in the yards and around the lake. All lights are on the trees by the first Friday in December, and they burn from then until the Sunday after Christmas. The lights are all in three traditional colors—red, white, and green. The sound of chimes floats from a church tower in the center of town, and many people enjoy simply walking about, looking at the trees, and listening to the music. A community celebration each year surrounds the Yule Log as it is dragged uphill amidst the caroling of the crowd and brought to burn in the fireplace of the Community Center.

In contrast to the consistency of the decoration of the trees, the doors of the houses are decorated in very individual ways. A contest with prizes encourages participation and ingenuity. Some individuals may cover an entire porch with a Christmas scene, while others may hang a single wreath. Most of the doorways have a small spotlight focused on them so the decorations are easily visible.

In McAdenville, an observer can enjoy two tours at once—a shared, community Christmas in the decoration of the trees and the individual interpretations of Christmas on the doorways.

Decorating for the Holidays

Decorating for the holidays is usually our announcement that the season has, indeed, arrived. The wreaths go up, the stockings are hung, the tree is decorated, candles are lit, and we are ready to celebrate the holiday with our family and friends.

Welcome returning family members and guests with an entryway that is all decked out for the season. Study the photographs in this chapter for ideas for wreaths, garlands, fanlight decorations, luminaries, even reindeer to graze across the yard. Then read the accompanying instructions to find what is behind the pretty front: what forms the bases of the different wreaths, what holds the apples in place on fanlight decorations, how to make the luminaries from our full-sized patterns, and how to assemble the reindeer.

Many of the indoor decorations can be completed early. Materials for the Vine Wreaths and the Nature Lover's Tree should be gathered and dried before the holiday season. The Tree of Ribbons, the Eucalyptus Wreath, Fire Starters, and Christmas Cardinals can all be leisurely finished in advance, and all of these will last throughout the season and beyond. Many of the projects are also quite inexpensive, relying on natural materials, candle stubs, paper, or ribbons that you make yourself. A Memory Tree, a room dressed in golden Scrolls & Ribbons, a tree in a dining room, and decorations for a Victorian tree—all of these offer simple but imaginative decorations for your tree as well as ideas for the whole room.

Start early to prepare the special touches that make your decorating plans really work for you. With the decorations in place, light the candles, sit back, and enjoy the warm Christmas atmosphere that you have created.

Spruce up the Outside

Fanlight Decorations

Fanlight decorations—like fanlights themselves—lend a stately appearance to an entryway. Fanlight decorations had their origins in the colonial period and can often be seen as seasonal displays in restorations of colonial homes (such as those in Colonial Williamsburg), but they should not be limited to restorations. Make one for your doorway as a welcoming symbol of good will to friend and stranger alike.

At the center of many fanlight decorations is a pineapple—a proud colonial symbol of hospitality and friendship. Two hundred years ago, tall ships travelled from the American colonies to the West Indies, trading staples like tar, turpentine, and barrel staves for sugar cane, rum, indigo, and coffee. Few captains could resist bringing back tropical fruits as well—and the most exotic of these was the juicy, yellow pineapple. The return trip took many weeks, however, and only a few of the perishable fruits would last that long. Those that did make it to the colonies were highly prized, and it was truly

a mark of high honor and friendship to be invited to share a pineapple. The pineapple gradually became so popular that it found its way into almost every form of colonial decoration—from the garden finials at Monticello to carvings on chests to stencils on walls and fabrics. When you post your pineapple above the door, take a moment to recall its forebears—and yours.

Fanlight decorations vary greatly in design and structure, but they share three characteristics: the use of locally available materials, simple styling, and a strong leaning toward symmetry. Let the directions given here for one decoration serve as a tool for understanding the basic structure, and then enjoy designing your own. And if you do not have a fanlight? Many homes are traditional enough in appearance so that they could have a fanlight decoration—if not a real fanlight—just for a season.

Begin to plan your own design by examining the natural materials you have available. Greenery usually forms the base of a design. All kinds of greenery combine well, from spiky blue-green spruce to glossy deep-green magnolia leaves. Choose fresh, long-lasting leaves or branches, and use them generously. Unblemished fruit—just slightly underripe, if possible—will last for several weeks if the weather is cool. Or, as shown in one of the photographs here, use pine cones in a stylized and symmetrical design. You will also need berries, pods, or smaller bits of greenery to complete the arrangement. Remember that this is the season for wind and rain, so you must carefully anchor the decoration. The appearance should be traditional, but concessions to the present in the form of materials to hold the arrangement in place will add to its stability.

This charming fanlight decoration is shaped precisely to fit its window.

A change in design may require some ingenuity in arranging new materials. Follow the principle of symmetry to use any of a wide number of natural materials—whatever is available to you in your area.

This over-the-door decoration is similar to a fanlight, but it can be made on a base of a long block of Styrofoam® strengthened by wrapping with wire and firmly secured to a window shelf. Heavy items must be carefully secured; then lighter greenery and berries can be added.

MATERIALS:
- **plywood**
- **pineapple**
- **tenpenny finishing nails**
- **18″ length thin wire**
- **7 screw eyes**
- **magnolia, aucuba, or rhododendron leaves**
- **staple gun and staples**
- **apples**
- **additional greenery and berries (optional)**
- **heavy duty wire**

To determine the size and shape of your finished fanlight arrangement, measure the width of the space over your door. Then measure how high you wish the decoration to stand in the space. Reduce both dimensions a bit to allow the tips of the background leaves to extend beyond the edges of the plywood. Cut a rectangle using the above dimensions; then cut the top into a symmetrical arch shape (A).

If the back of the plywood will be visible from the inside of the house, cover it with evergreen leaves, stapling them into a fan shape as described below.

The symmetry that is such an appealing aspect of this design requires careful planning. Choose apples that are consistent in size. With the photograph as a guide, arrange several of the apples along the curve of the plywood until you are pleased with the spacing between them. Measure the distance between the centers of two adjacent apples. Use this as a standard measurement in spacing rows and in spacing the apples along the rows.

Mark the vertical center of the plywood. Place the pineapple at the center bottom; draw around the general outline of the pineapple with a pencil to mark the space it will require (A).

Following the contour of the curved edge of the plywood, draw a line 5″ inside the outer edge. Draw other lines for rows of apples parallel with the first line and spaced so that the distance between lines is equal to your measurement between apples (A).

Drive one finishing nail at the center of the line that marks the top row of apples, slanting the head of this and all other nails toward the top. Working from this center nail to each side, space other finishing nails along the curved line at intervals that correspond to your standard measurement. For the rows that are broken by the outline of the pineapple, place a finishing nail 2″ to the right of the pineapple outline. Measure from that nail to the center line. Place another finishing nail to the left at the same distance from the center line. Working from these two nails, space other finishing nails at standard intervals along the line. Follow this procedure to position nails for additional rows of apples (B).

Working within the outline of the pineapple, place 2 finishing nails, also slanting upward, beneath the fruit (B). Place one screw eye in the center of the outline of the pineapple leaves. Attach an 18″ length of wire to the screw eye (B).

Attach a screw eye 2″ from the top center of the plywood and a screw eye 2″ from each bottom corner. Wrap heavy-duty wire through the screw eyes, twisting tightly, and extend the wires away from the form (B).

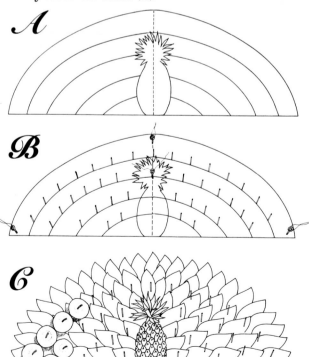

A

B

C

16

A garland can enhance the effectiveness of the decoration.

Clip the stiff, unwieldy stem ends from magnolia, aucuba, or rhododendron leaves. Staple the leaves along the outside of the plywood, extending the leaves over the edge of the plywood. Staple rows of leaves in additional curved lines, one row inside the other and with ends of leaves overlapping the staples, to cover the plywood (C). (It will be necessary to puncture some leaves with nails to cover evenly.)

Impale apples on the rows of nails, their stems pointing forward. Impale the pineapple on its nails. Twist the wire beneath the pineapple top around the leaves to secure them firmly in place. Staple on additional greenery or berries.

Attach 3 screw eyes to window in positions corresponding with those on the fanlight arrangement. Holding the fanlight in position, tightly twist the wires that are at top and sides of arrangement through the screw eyes on the house. Check to be sure that the arrangement is completely secure.

A Southern Welcome

A magnificent doorway deserves a magnificent decoration for the holidays. The entrance to the home of the President of Auburn University is graced with a wreath and garland of magnolia leaves interspersed with clusters of whitened nandina berries—the berries adding their own dignified accent to the traditional white house.

The wreath is made on a base of a straw wreath form wrapped with strips of green plastic. The stems of the magnolia leaves are wired to florist's picks and poked into the wreath. Clusters of nandina berries are simply dipped in white house paint, drained over newspapers, and, when they are dry, wired to florist's picks and added to the wreath. A white bow is also attached with a florist's pick.

The garland, because it is fairly heavy and contains so many branches of magnolia, requires a substantial support. The designer fashioned an arched support of chicken wire, 6" wide and the length of the garland. The sharp edges of the wire were rolled inward, and the magnolia branches were pushed into the wire base to form a thick garland around the door. Clusters of white berries were wired to florist's picks and added to the garland.

Cotton Boll Wreath

The cotton boll wreath is a natural for Southerners. The quiet shades of beige and brown create an appearance of overall softness—a pleasant contrast to the traditional wreath of green. Swirled and tucked, the plaid ribbon with its threads of gold further enhances the natural beauty of this wreath.

MATERIALS:
    straw wreath form
    wire for hanger
    large bag of cotton bolls
    florist's picks
    4 yards (¾"-wide) plaid ribbon

Wrap wire around the straw wreath at the top and form a loop for hanging. Attach each boll to a florist's pick. Slanting the picks, insert them into the straw wreath. Keeping in mind that the finished wreath should appear airy, continue to insert the picks, working in the same direction around the wreath. Swirl and tuck the ribbon; no pins are necessary.

Reindeer

These reindeer grazing across the yard are a joy to passersby, but they are the most fun to their builders—who discover the personalities of their deer as they find and assemble the parts. To make true reindeer, you must first go for a walk in their world. Logs for heads and bodies may be as close as your woodpile, but if you do find large parts there, you will still want to traipse to the woods for a wide choice of legs, neck, and antlers.

To find all the materials for your deer, get the family together and head for a nice wooded area with both pine and hardwood trees. The main body of your deer should be about 3' long and 6" to 9" in diameter. The best material is a standing dead pine tree; you don't want to cut a live one, but you don't want a decayed one either. The head can come from the same tree; it should be about 8" to 12" long and 4" to 6" in diameter. The legs are best if they can be cut from hardwood; a pole that is 2½' long and 1½" in diameter will be just right. Cut an extra length for a neck, about a foot long. The antlers will be hiding in the branches around you, but you must find two that are similar in shape, strong but not too heavy. The tail can be made of pampas grass or a twig—whatever fits your deer.

Lay the body of the deer on its back. With a 1" bit, drill four holes at a 45-degree angle to bottom center of body. (Drill all holes at least 1½" deep.) With a knife, taper the ends of the legs and drive them into the holes. Stand the deer and adjust the height of the legs with a saw so that the deer is well balanced.

The neck hole can be positioned on the top or on the cut end of the body, depending upon the log you have chosen and upon whether the deer is to be nibbling at grass or alert to passersby. Taper the neck at both ends and mount the head. If the tail is to be a twig or small branch, drill a hole for it and insert into the body. Drill 2 holes for the antlers and wiggle them into place.

The Birds' Gift

Share the spirit of Christmas with feathered friends by making this bread dough and birdseed wreath. Hang it on a door or window during the holidays. Later set it outside as a holiday feast for the birds.

MATERIALS:
  3 individual loaves frozen bread dough
    (Regular bread dough is also suitable,
    as long as it makes enough for 3
    loaves.)
  picture hanging wire
  egg white
  birdseed
  ribbon

Thaw the bread dough on a floured surface. Stretch each loaf as evenly as possible to a length of approximately 30″. This may be a little difficult because the dough is elastic and tries to return to its original shape. Allow one end of each length to hang over the edge of the counter; its own weight will keep it from shrinking.

Pinch the three pieces together firmly at one end. Braid the lengths; then form a circle with the ends attached to each other. Imbed a loop of picture wire deeply into the back of the dough. This will later be used as a hanger.

Place the braided circle on a large greased cookie sheet; allow it to rise according to directions on the package of bread dough. Bake at the recommended temperature until just slightly brown. Remove from oven, and brush top and sides thickly with beaten egg white. Sprinkle birdseed on top before the egg white dries. Bake a few more minutes to complete browning.

Some seeds will fall off when the wreath is moved, but you can add more by using more eggwhite and resprinkling.

Allow the wreath to dry out and become hard for several days before you attempt to hang it. Attach a bow to the wreath with straight pins and tuck in bits of greenery.

After the wreath has graced your door for the season, remove the bow and its pins, and place in a quiet area of the yard.

Favorite Things

Welcome guests this party season with a vignette of well-loved keepsakes. Trunks, quilts, logs, greenery, horns, dolls. All of these stir nostalgic appreciation for the traditions and pleasures of Christmas. Take your treasures from their boxes, and arrange a special greeting for a party; after the party, bring the collection into the family room for the holidays.

Luminaries

Herald the season with luminaries to cheer arriving guests. Angels, stars, and trees proclaim the season as they light the way to your door. Luminaries are a traditional Christmas decoration of the Southwest. The source of the light is a candle, and, as with any open flame, precautions must be taken to avoid fires. Remove accumulations of leaves from the area of the luminaries. Be sure paper bags are stiff enough not to blow into the flame. Anchor bags and candles carefully with plenty of sand, and do not leave the luminaries unattended for any length of time.

MATERIALS:
   patterns on pages 135-137
   grocery sacks
   white typing paper
   green and yellow tissue paper
   white household glue
   sand
   votive candles

For tree and star, trace patterns (pages 135-137) onto typing paper, one tracing along outside lines and one along heavier inside lines. Cut out tracings. Position inside (smaller) pattern on one side of a grocery sack and draw around it. To prevent cutting the back of the sack, place a piece of heavy cardboard inside sack. Using a craft knife, cut along the lines you have drawn.

For the tree, draw around the outside (larger) pattern on green tissue paper and cut out. For the star, use the large tracing.

Glue the typing paper star or the green tissue tree over the corresponding cutouts on sacks, overlapping edges evenly on all sides.

For the angel, three tracings are required. Using the angel pattern, make these 3 tracings on typing paper: one along the outside lines, one along the heavier lines that are just inside the lines used for the first tracing, and one along the "keyhole" or inside lines that form the angel's head and dress. Cut out the three tracings.

Place the pattern traced from the heavier lines on a grocery sack, and draw around it. Cut out the shape as described above.

Draw around the first (largest) pattern on yellow tissue paper and cut out. Run a thin line of glue around the edges of the cutout on the sack. Glue tissue-paper angel over the cutout on the sack, with edges overlapping evenly on all sides.

Run a thin line of glue around the edges of the third (keyhole) tracing. Place this on top of yellow tissue-paper angel, centering the head inside the halo. Fold top of sack twice for a cuff. Add enough sand to stabilize the luminary, and set candle firmly into the sand.

Golden Harvest Wreath

A harvest wreath rich with the golds of Autumn is perfectly displayed against the warm browns of a wooden door. Wheat, corn, and okra pods take a golden turn for a striking alternative to the simple clusters of Indian corn adorning many entrances in the fall.

MATERIALS:
  rainbow corn (Indian corn)
  strawberry ornamental corn
  dried okra pods
  wheat
  metallic gold spray paint
  1 (16″-diameter) wire wreath form
  1 spool 22-gauge brass wire

Completely cover the wheat, dried okra pods, strawberry and Indian corn with gold spray paint, being careful not to spray the husks of the corn. Allow to dry.

Begin wiring the Indian corn to the wire wreath form, working in one direction around the form. Overlap the ears and husks so that the entire wreath form is covered by the Indian corn.

Wire strawberry corn together in groups of two or three and wire to the wreath form by poking the wire through the husks of the Indian corn. Poke holes through the okra pods, wire together in clusters, and position around the wreath.

Tuck wheat into the wreath as accents.

The Golden Harvest Wreath is unusually heavy and the corn will tend to shift a bit as the wreath is moved. Once in position on your door, simply tuck the ears into place. A bit more wiring may need to be done once it is hung, and you may wish to trim a few of the more unruly husks for a more symmetrical appearance.

Seashell Wreath

Seashells, with their own delicate, natural symmetry and exquisite colorations, can be made into a durable wreath that is undaunted by winter wind and rain. With the addition of a garland of greenery, this doorway reflects a collector's passion and bids a distinctive welcome to the season.

MATERIALS:
  1 spool florist's wire
  15″-diameter straw wreath form
  electric drill and 1/16″ bit
  12 (3″ to 4″) round, flat, colored shells
    (such as China red moon)
  1 package U-shaped florist's pins
  white household glue
  12 (2″ to 3″) white pectin shells (such as
    Japanese cups)
  1 large bunch twigs or other filler
  bow

Cut a 4′ length of florist's wire and double it. Wrap it around the wreath form several times, and form a loop to hang the wreath, twisting the loop to secure it tightly. Trim excess wire.

Place a large, flat, colored shell round side down on a scrap piece of board. (You will drill on the inside of the shell cup.) Grasp the shell firmly with one hand. Using an electric drill with a 1/16″ bit, drill 2 holes in the shell, spacing the holes

about ⅜" apart and 1" from the base. Drill holes in each of the remaining colored shells.

Place drilled shells on wreath at an equal distance from each other. A shell should be placed directly over the wire that is at the center top. Stick one U-shaped florist's pin through each shell to secure it to the wreath.

Apply glue to the inside edge of each white pectin shell and allow to dry until the glue feels tacky. Press the pectin shells on top of the flat, colored shells, covering the U-shaped florist's

pins and aligning the shell bases.

Cover the straw wreath by attaching twigs to inside and outside edges of the wreath form and between shells with the U-shaped florist's pins. Attach bow to wreath with wire.

Special Touches for the House

A Victorian Christmas

Christmas celebrations took on a special lavishness in the Victorian era. Elaborate preparations for the holidays were met with enthusiastic response. The opulence of the period, however, was often an opulence of style rather than of expense. The Victorian enthusiasm for handwork was exceeded only by the enthusiasm for thrift and using the last scrap of cloth or paper. Handwork and thrift were combined to produce numerous gifts, ornaments, and decorations that were unique to their era.

The Victorian tree, for example, was a grand production, but many of the decorations were made from paper, cards, cotton, even the peel of an orange. So many of the decorations for a Victorian Christmas can be made as family projects and a Victorian tree seems especially to welcome the contributions of children. Strings of popcorn, paper chains, fans, favorite cards—all of these are easy to make and virtually free!

The traditions, decorations, and foods of a Victorian Christmas are collected in *The Gift of Christmas Past A Return to Victorian Traditions* by Sunny O'Neil and available through the American Association for State and Local History, 703 Berry Road, Nashville, TN 37204.

A COBWEB PARTY

The distribution of presents in the Victorian household was carefully planned and merrily executed. Always on the lookout for novel ways of presenting the gifts, many Victorian mothers quickly adopted the idea of the cobweb party when it appeared in *Saint Nicholas* magazine in December 1876.

The cobweb party shown here was photographed in the nineteenth-century Arlington Historic House in Birmingham, Alabama. Here we can see just how the party would have looked in its Victorian setting, but the same idea could be adapted to a family room of today.

The idea of the cobweb is simple. You need a ball of string or yarn in a different color for each member of the family. Tie the presents for one person to the same color of string. Beginning at the back of the room, tie the strings to the heaviest presents. Crisscross the strings around the room, looping around chair legs or over curtain rods, making a colorful web of the strings. Lightweight presents or ornaments can be suspended from the strings. The strings can also go beneath cushions where small presents are hidden. Heavy presents can be attached to the strings but resting on furniture or floor. All strings should end at the doorway and be attached to strips of cardboard for rewinding.

When all is ready, the originator of the idea, in her letter to *Saint Nicholas*, suggests that the mother lead the way to the room, reciting:

"Will you come into my parlor?"
Said the spider to the fly.
"Tis the prettiest little parlor that ever you did
    spy;
The way into my parlor is up a winding stair,
And I have many pretty things to show you
    when you're there.
Will you, will you, walk in, Mister Fly?"

Allow a few minutes for appreciative inspection of the intricate arrangement and guessing about eventual rewards. Then hand each family member his spool and watch the excitement as the string is rewound and the gifts are discovered.

GOOD FORTUNE CHAIN

For a tree of good fortune and happy wishes for the New Year, drape the tree with a paper chain of hidden predictions. Fortunes and good wishes are revealed only when the chain is broken—what a perfect game for a Twelfth Night party when friends gather to help take down the Christmas tree. Each person takes a turn to break a link and read his or her fortune aloud.

MATERIALS:
  wrapping paper, colored on one side,
    white on the other
  white household glue
  gold paper

Cut strips of paper 4″ × 1″. On the white side of the strips, write fortunes or special wishes. Make a chain of loops of the fortune strips with glue. Add gold links at each end of the fortune chain so that the "fortune" sections will be easy to find. Then add links without fortunes to complete a chain long enough to garland your tree. (Any person ambitious enough to write fortunes on all the links for the whole garland will surely prosper in the coming year!)

PEANUT GARLAND

This garland, an excellent example of the Victorian use of materials on hand, uses peanuts as the shapers beneath the tissue paper.

MATERIALS:
  peanuts in shell
  various colors of tissue paper
  gold thread

Cut tissue paper into 4" squares. Fringe two ends by clipping along the edges. Roll the paper around a peanut and twist the fringed ends. Tie the gold cord around the middle of the peanut, leave a 3½" length of cord, tie on another peanut, and so on, making a garland as long as you wish. Three or four peanuts may also be strung together to hang vertically as an individual ornament for the tree.

ORANGE BASKET

Sweet-treat baskets are fashioned from orange peels to hold candied orange peel and other nibbles—high in the branches of a Victorian Christmas tree.

MATERIALS:
  orange
  16" (¼"-wide) orange ribbon
  **candied orange peel (see recipe for
    Candied Citrus Peel, page 106)**

Cut two wedges of peel from the orange so that a ½"-wide strip for the handle remains attached to the bottom half of the orange. Save the peel from the wedges to be candied. Scoop out the fruit and place the basket in a warm place to dry. Drying time will vary from one to two weeks.

Wrap a narrow ribbon around the dried basket, as shown in the photograph, and tie a bow at the top. Fill with candied orange peel or other lightweight candies.

COTTON SANTA AND LADY

The cotton ornaments shown here were inspired by those imported from Germany in the 1880s. They look substantial but are actually very lightweight.

MATERIALS:
  cutouts of faces and figures
  cardboard
  cotton
  white household glue
  various trims
  thread for hanger

Cut out face or figure from wrapping paper or an old Christmas card. Cut a cardboard backing to make a "body" for the face. The shapes are very simple; imagine only the outlines of the ornaments in the photograph. Glue the face onto the cardboard. Glue pieces of cotton (or bright fabric for the Victorian lady) here and there to look like fur or a beard. Add other adornments as you wish: felt hands, a feather on a hat, twigs for Santa. Glue a hanger of thread on the back.

Nature Lover's Tree

Subtle colorations of natural seedpods and dried flowers provide a pleasant, old-fashioned counterpoint to the usual holiday red and green. This spectacular tree will last throughout the season—and beyond—though it can be made well ahead of time when plant materials can be gathered at the peak of their color. Various flowers or ribbons may be added to harmonize with your own room. Beginning with the largest cone of Styrofoam® that is available, the tree may be extended to any size you need by adding larger and larger rounds of Styrofoam® to the bottom of the cone.

MATERIALS:
   **dried materials: baby's breath,
      hydrangeas, broom bloom, goldenrod,
      teasel, pine cones, etc.
   large Styrofoam® cone and disks in
      increasing diameter sizes to stack to
      desired tree height
   toothpicks
   white household glue
   medium brown flat spray paint
   florist's picks
   florist's wire
   ribbon**

Collect dried materials for the tree from late spring through early fall. Some materials, such as hydrangeas, can be allowed to dry directly on the bush. Goldenrod should be picked in full bloom and hung in a dry, dark place—dry to prevent rotting and dark to retain as much color as possible. Other plants that can be air dried and used for the tree include baby's breath, tansy, yarrow, strawflower, statice, and lunaria. Bleach and dyes can be used to color some dried materials; the materials must then be dried again.

Place the Styrofoam® cone on top of a stack of Styrofoam® disks of graduated sizes to make a base of the desired height. Secure the layers to each other with several toothpicks that have been dipped in glue.

Spray the entire cone base with the medium brown spray paint, and allow to dry.

Attach the dried flowers to florist's picks. Twist pieces of wire around the pine cones. Cut ribbons into 8" lengths. Form bows from 8" lengths of ribbon and fasten to a florist's pick.

Dip the ends of the wires of the pine cones into glue and place them randomly on the tree. Fill in most of the remaining space with hydrangeas. Add baby's breath, broom bloom, goldenrod, teasels, and ribbons until you have covered the tree shape.

Eucalyptus Wreath

Warm and lovely, a eucalyptus wreath is suitable for almost any room in the home, regardless of the decor—formal or informal, contemporary or country. Although it gives pleasure in any season, this wreath is especially nice at Christmas when it adds to the wonderful smells of the holiday season.

MATERIALS:
   **wire for hanger
   15" straw wreath form
   3 or 4 bunches of eucalyptus
   florist's picks with wires
   5 deodar cedar cones
   bow**

Wrap wire around the straw wreath at the top and form a loop for hanging. Cut the eucalyptus branches into sprigs, varying the lengths from 4" to 6". (To make an attractive tip for each sprig, cut very closely to the top of the pair of leaves that will be the new "top" of a stem.) Gather three or four sprigs into a cluster. Wrap the wire from a florist's pick around the cluster. Insert the cluster into the straw wreath at an angle. Working in the same direction around the wreath form, fill in the front and sides until all the straw is concealed. Wrap the wire of a florist's pick around each of the deodar cones and add to the wreath. Attach a bow with a florist's pick.

A Quiet Celebration

Who says a Christmas tree must be in the family room? This Douglas fir is resplendent in the dining room with marbelized eggs, eggs with scenes painted on them, golden fans, and other ornaments made by friends. An angel in flowing robes tops the tree.

The table is set for a party with an arrangement of boxwood and pink sweetheart roses. Small holiday "favors" are wrapped to repeat the pastel tones of the china, and across the room, a vine wreath frames a mirror.

METALLIC FOIL FANS

Cut 12" × 16" pieces of foil, fold in half lengthwise (to 6" × 16"), and pleat. With a hole puncher, make holes through the pinched end of the pleated fan. Thread ribbon through and tie in a bow.

TREE TOP ANGEL

The huge Christmas tree at the Metropolitan Museum of Art in New York City is traditionally covered with eighteenth-century Italian terra cotta and wooden angels. It was these glorious angels that inspired our designer to make the gentle tree top angel shown here. This one was made from a doll of the 1940s with a ceramic head and cloth body, but—for such a coveted position—any 6" doll would love to change her clothes, at least for one holiday season.

MATERIALS:

pattern for wings, page 136
6" doll
¼ yard blue silk taffeta
4" × 20" strip of pink silk taffeta
gold cord
2 (15" × 6") pieces gold foil wrapping paper
white household glue
tinsel pipe cleaner
tiny gold ornament

For the skirt, cut a piece of blue fabric 8½" × 16"; sew the ends together to form a tube. Turn under a hem and stitch. Turn under ½" and sew running stitches around the top. Gather the skirt around the waistline of the doll and tack to hold.

For the overdress, cut a piece of blue fabric 4½" × 15" and hem the raw edges. Cut a small hole for the neck opening and hem the raw edges around the hole. Place the overdress over the head of the doll and wrap with the gold cord around the waist and over the shoulders, crisscrossing on the bodice and tying in the back.

For the flowing robe, cut a piece of pink fabric 4" × 20" long. Taper the ends. Hem the raw edges. Wrap around one arm of the doll and tack with needle and thread. Bunch up the fabric to give a rich, rumpled look. Tack the robe to the side of the skirt to hold the folds in place.

For the wings, cut 2 (15" × 6") pieces of gold foil wrapping paper. Glue the pieces back to back so that the foil shows on both sides. Fold in half crosswise. Trace the wing pattern on page 136, and use as a pattern to cut out the wings. Pin the wings to the back of the angel's dress.

Form a circle of a tinsel pipe cleaner and place on the angel's head for a halo. String a small gold ornament on a cord for the incense burner.

A graceful grapevine wreath encircles a mirror for the holidays. (See page 44 for instructions on making a vine wreath.) Bittersweet and berries are woven into the wreath for added color, and, for very special occasions, four rubrum lilies—kept fresh in plastic water vials—are tucked in.

MARBELIZED & PAINTED EGGS

MATERIALS:
    blown eggs
    10″ wooden or bamboo skewers
    model paint in gold and silver and
      various colors
    metallic tinsel or colored pipe cleaners

For marbelized eggs, blow out the contents of the eggs. Mount the egg on a thin wooden skewer by wrapping a small rubber band around the skewer, threading the egg onto the skewer, and adding another rubber band at the other end of the egg. This will keep the egg from slipping off the skewer.

Fill a plastic container ⅔ full of water and add 3 to 4 drops of paint to the surface of the water. (A very little paint goes a long way.) Swirl the paint over the surface with a skewer. If you are using gold or silver metallic paint, drip this paint on top of a film of colored paint already on the water. The metallic paints are too heavy to float; a layer of color will keep them on the surface long enough to coat the egg. Swirl paint to make a marblelike pattern.

Plunge the egg immediately into the water, submerging it and pulling it right out again. Let any excess water drain out of the egg, and stand the skewer upright in a jar until the paint dries.

Skim any excess paint from the surface of the water before doing another egg. To hang the eggs, thread a pipe cleaner through the holes of the eggs. Make a loop at each end or arrange the pipe cleaner into a bow. You may trim the eggs with ribbons, metallic cord, and tiny ornaments.

For painted eggs, use the same technique to mount the egg on a skewer. With a fine paint brush, paint the egg with the model paint except for an oval area for the scene. Let the paint dry. Paint a favorite holiday scene. (Our designer used a Christmas tree on a hill of snow with blue sky above.) When the scene is dry, paint a garland of gold or silver around the edge. Mount the egg on a pipe cleaner and trim as desired.

Herbs of Christmas

A garden of Christmas herbs is a charming way to share the season with a friend. Take the herbs from your own garden in the fall and set them into an indoor decorative arrangement for the winter; they provide the foundation for a new herb garden for your friend in the spring.

Herbs have long been valued for their flavor, aroma, or medicinal properties—but this only begins to explain our fascination with the individual herbs that have taken on a symbolism of their own. The particular herbs in this holiday gift basket have, through the centuries, acquired meanings specifically related to Christmas.

Rosemary is the principal herb of Christmas and a symbol of remembrance. According to legend, rosemary once had only white flowers. During the flight to Egypt, the Holy Family took shelter near the fragrant shrub. After washing Baby Jesus's swaddling clothes and her own blue cloak in a running brook, Mary spread the garments on the fragrant branches of flowering rosemary to dry. When she removed the garments, they had taken on the fragrance of the herb, and the white flowers had changed to blue. During the Middle Ages, sprigs of rosemary were placed in babies' cradles to insure safe, peaceful sleep.

Rue, called by Shakespeare "the Herb of Grace," is a symbol of virtue. It has been reputed to banish evil spirits and to bestow second sight.

Thyme is considered a manger herb and is a symbol of courage, activity, and bravery.

Alpine strawberries are symbols of true worth, the blossom a symbol of foresight, and the whole plant a symbol of perfect excellence.

Sage is symbolic of domestic virtue and immortality: "Ye who eats his sage in May, will live for aye."

Horehound, one of the bitter herbs of Passover, was thought also to have been mixed with the sweet herbs and grasses of the manger.

Other plants shown in this basket garden include aloe, ivy, and nasturtium. *Aloe*, the ancient symbol of affection, was one of the sources of the precious oils brought by the three kings. Twined about the handle of the basket are *ivy*, the symbol of love and friendship, and *nasturtium*, symbol of truth and splendor.

MATERIALS:
cuttings of herbs
sphagnum moss
basket
plastic bowl to line basket

About six weeks before the holidays, take cuttings of herbs from outdoors. Soak the moss in water. Place the plastic liner in the basket. Fill with the wet moss. Set the cuttings 1″ to 2″ into the moss. Add a cutting of twining ivy or nasturtium, perhaps a bow.

Attach a small tag of care instructions to the gift baskets, including the following information: The cuttings will do better in a cool, sunny location. Mist the garden daily. A light fertilizing with a water soluble fertilizer every six weeks is also helpful. The cuttings should take root by spring. Then, to start your own garden outside, pull the herbs gently from the moss and place in pots. When the plants are strong and healthy, usually in three to four weeks, they can be transplanted into the garden.

Goodie String

In the home of a yeoman farmer of the mid-nine-teenth century South, the Goodie String pro-vided both a seasonal decoration and a

hospitable gesture. It was customary for vis-iting children to be of-fered a treat of their choice from the Good-ie String. The antebel-lum tradition of the Goodie String is docu-mented and shared with us through the Tullie Smith House Restoration, one of the few pre-Civil War houses standing in the Atlanta area. Built about 1840, the house is restored to reflect the life of a yeoman farmer of the period. The Goodie String, photographed in the detached kitchen where family and friends would gather about the hearth for meals and visits, can be duplicated by following the directions below.

MATERIALS:
   13 yards heavy tan mailing cord
   20 pecans
   20 peanuts
   1 quart popped popcorn
   6 sugar cookies
   small package dried apricots
   6 chestnuts
   5 small apples
   small amount of yarn

Make a continuous 36"-diameter circle of the mailing cord, reserving 1 yard of cord for tying on the nuts. Cut once across the cords to make individual lengths. In the center of the cords, tie a knot; this knot becomes the top of the goodie string. Braid tightly from this knot to the end of the cords. Tie off with a short piece of cord.

With an electric drill, drill holes through one end of the pecans. String the pecans together in groups of five and tie into a loop. Tie with cord to the goodie string.

String peanuts, four or five together, with nee-dle and thread. Tie in a bunch, and tie to goodie string with cord.

String popcorn with needle and thread to about a 10" string, make a loop and tie off, and attach to goodie string.

Prepare sugar cookies. When they come from the oven, use a drinking straw to make a hole at one side. Cool cookies, slip yarn through hole, and tie to braid.

String dried apricots in groups of 2 or 3 with a large-eyed needle and a loop of string or yarn, and attach to braid.

Drill holes through the chestnuts and attach to the braid singly with string.

On the stem side, impale apples halfway onto 1¼" aluminum nail. Insert the head of the nail in the braid.

A Great Idea Set a festive mood in the kitchen with an imaginative countertop creation. Arrange candles with an assortment of metal cooking utensils such as graters, molds, and steamers. Add cinnamon sticks, ribbon, and sprigs of holly or other greenery. Light the candles and enjoy the glow.

Memory Tree

Family Memories—vacations, parties, holidays, family reunions, weddings, birthdays, anniversaries, ballet recitals, home runs—can be turned into treasured medallions for your Christmas tree. This busy family's tree is laden with hand-painted glimpses into the adventure they shared on their many travels.

The tree skirt also reflects the extensive travel that is a part of the life of this family. Family members in felt, bags in hand, are glued onto a white background. A boat, plane, train, and car define the ways that the family travels. Begin your memory tree now and add to the collection every year.

MATERIALS:
3" circles (⅛"-thick) plywood
white enamel paint
acrylics or fine point markers
fishing line for hangers

Drill a small hole in the top of the plywood circles. Paint circles with white enamel, covering the front, back, and sides. Sketch your "memory" onto the circle. Paint the scene with acrylics or fine point markers. Add a title. On the back, write names and dates. Make a hanger of fishing line.

Tree of Ribbons

Beautiful, long-lasting, and economical—this tree is all of these. You can make your own ribbons of any calico design you choose.

MATERIALS:
calico in 2 or 3 patterns
20-gauge wire
15"-high cone of Styrofoam®
wooden goblet or other base

Make your own ribbons from scraps of calico by starching the fabric as stiff as possible, ironing it smooth, and cutting into ½"-wide strips.

Cut the strips into 14" lengths. Notch the ends of the lengths of ribbon. Fold into a bow shape, and twist a 3" length of wire around the bow.

Insert the bows into the cone, covering the cone completely and using the different calicoes in clusters for a patchwork effect. Place the cone on the base.

Note: For a 24-page booklet of designer Sunny O'Neil's *Favorite Christmas Decorations*, send $2.00 (postpaid) to Sunny O'Neil, 7106 River Road, Bethesda, MD 20034.

A bow is such a simple thing, but when it is made of metallic ribbon and repeated over a whole tree, it becomes an exciting decorative motif.

42

Scrolls & Ribbons

A room that dazzles the eye with the glitter of Christmas gold! The warmth and sophistication achieved with simple touches of gold ribbon and paper suit the everyday elegance of this living room and its furnishings and complement the color scheme in a way that traditional reds and greens would not. Add the flicker of candles in the evening to give a luster to the whole room.

The tree has as its only ornaments gold balls, tiny white lights, and simple bows made of embossed gold foil ribbons. The tree topper is a large, puffy bow of a wider embossed foil ribbon, and streamers from the top help to give shape and definition to the tree. Packages are wrapped in white tissue and gold foil and tied with the same ribbon that is used on the tree.

GOLDEN SCROLLS

The "trees" on the mantel and the doorway scrolls are made from the same pattern. The shapes can be saved from year to year and used on a buffet or table or in front of a large mirror.

MATERIALS:
pattern on page 138
double-sided metallic gold poster board
rubber cement or spray made for
   mounting prints
craft knife

Both sides of the poster board must be gold. If you cannot find double-sided board, use rubber cement or mounting spray to attach two pieces of single-sided board to each other.

Enlarge the pattern on page 138 to full size, and cut out. Trace around the pattern on the poster board. Using a craft knife, carefully cut out the shape. Repeat to make as many pieces as needed for your individual display. The doorway decoration requires four shapes simply arranged around the door.

These fanciful shapes of gold poster board can add interest around windows as well as doors.

Each "tree" requires a minimum of four scroll shapes. With a hole punch, make 4 holes down the straight edge of each scroll shape. Loosely tie the shapes together with a small piece of gold cord through each of the 4 sets of holes. Place the shapes upright and fan out for a full tree shape.

A vine wreath with gold paper leaves is hung over a mantel that is covered with greenery and gold balls and balanced with the golden sculptured trees that are described on the preceding page.

VINE WREATH

A classic vine wreath can be used throughout the year with many embellishments. The materials are free and widely available; as a matter of fact, the vines often need to be cut back. The wreath you make this year can be changed with the seasons and the years. See page 36 for another vine wreath with a different appearance.

MATERIALS:
   honeysuckle, grapevine, or kudzu vines
   gold paper leaves

Loop a long, thick vine into a circle the size you want the wreath to be. Loop another vine around the first. Continue to wrap the vine around and through the wreath until the wreath is thick and full. No ties are necessary; simply tuck the ends of each of the vines into the wreath shape to secure.

Attach the gold paper leaves by twisting their wire stems onto the vines, positioning the leaves in the same direction around the wreath.

Simple clay figures handmade in Mexico are effectively displayed without a stable. Delicate baby's breath and lacy straw mats unify the entire scene and provide a creamy "halo" around the rustic figures.

The Crèche

In a quiet area of the home, the crèche awaits the contemplative moments of the season. Children enjoy the miniature portrayal of the story their parents tell or read to them, and this symbol of the family gathering often becomes a treasured family heirloom, linking one generation to another. Many families begin with one crèche, discover another that seems just as appealing, then add perhaps a third—and find themselves collectors of the varying forms of crèches.

The tradition of the crèche, or Nativity scene, was popularized by St. Francis of Assisi who used live animals and human actors to portray the Christmas story. Living crèches are still popular in many places. Stone Mountain, Georgia, and Bethlehem, Kentucky, for example, each year re-enact the story of Jesus's birth. Other living nativity scenes—neither famous nor regularly staged—may be happened upon in an evening's drive around your town.

The family crèche portrays the same scene of the Nativity in smaller size and in an astonishing array of materials from around the world: carved wood from Germany, straw from Ecuador, glass from Italy, olivewood from Bethlehem, clay from Colombia. There are also crèches of pewter and porcelain, of paper and fabric, of papier-mâche and stained glass.

Because they are in miniature, the figures can seem lost in the stronger colors and motifs of Christmas. The materials from which your crèche is made may even seem inconsistent with the room setting. In the Nativity scenes shown here, backdrops have been devised to set a stage for the crèches and to set them off from their surroundings. Holly and other fresh greenery of the season are favorite backgrounds for displaying a crèche, but other effective settings may also be fashioned. Several yards of fabric may be draped from a point high above the crèche—perhaps marked by a large Star of Bethlehem. The fluffy beige plumes of pampas grass or spiky palm fronds are also imaginative backgrounds.

A treasured Nativity scene made of plaster and purchased in Germany many years ago needs only a backdrop of Christmas greenery to highlight the subtle shades and gentle features of the figures.

Christmas Cardinals

A gathering of bright red cardinals is sure to warm the most wintry day. These jaunty paper birds can perch on a bare branch as shown here or they can spruce up a tree or package.

MATERIALS:
> **pattern on page 135**
> **heavy red paper (preferably with a glossy coating)**
> **black marking pen**
> **red tissue paper**
> **white household glue**

Your paper must be red on both sides; two pieces can be glued together if you are unable to find double-sided red paper.

Trace the pattern given on page 135, and cut out your paper pattern. Place the body pattern on the heavy red paper, and draw around it to transfer the bird shape to the paper. Cut out the bird shape. With the pattern as a guide, draw the beak and the eye onto the bird with a black marking pen.

From the red tissue paper, cut one wing (6" × 4½") and one tail (5½" × 2½"). Pleat each of these, running the folds across the shorter side of each wing and tail piece and making the pleats very narrow.

Place the pleated tail in place on the body of the bird. Lift the first pleat on each side of the tail, and staple through the other pleats and bird body. Push the top pleats in place to conceal the staple.

Cut slits in the body for the wing as indicated on the pattern. Slide the pleated wing through the slit. Pull the back edges of each side of the wing to meet the body. Use a very small amount of glue along these last pleats, and hold the wings against the body until the tissue sticks to the body of the bird. Spread the wings.

46

Counting the Days

The days between the time the stockings are hung and the night Santa finally comes sometimes seem agonizingly long for a child. Hang the stockings December 1, but let these bright, numbered streamers of paper ribbon help an excited child count off the days until Christmas. Cut 24 (30″-long) pieces of ribbon. Tie one end of each of 23 ribbons around a piece of wrapped candy. Sandwich the other end of each ribbon between two small gummed labels from the stationery counter, and number the labels from 1 to 23. Label a 24th ribbon and tie it to a special unbreakable ornament for the tree—perhaps a star. Place the ornament and candy-laden ends of the ribbon streamers inside the stocking, beginning with the larger numbers and allowing the smaller numbers to rest on top to avoid tangles. Each day the child can remove the numbered ribbon that corresponds with the date. When the special ornament is taken from the stocking and placed on the tree, it will be Christmas Eve and the stocking will be empty just in time for Santa's full attention.

Fire Starters

A basket of pine cone fire starters is a pleasant promise of cozy nights to come. Keep some on your hearth, and make extras for gifts. You need only medium-sized pine cones, paraffin or candle stubs, wicking or wicks from the stubs, red and green crayons, and muffin tins. Make sure pine cones are dry and fully opened. (Open partially closed cones by baking them 30 minutes in a 200°F. oven.) Be sure bottoms of cones will fit into muffin cups.

Melt paraffin or candle stubs in a double boiler over hot water. Do not place boiler directly on the heat, as paraffin has a very low flash point and may catch fire. Dip each cone in paraffin to coat completely; remove and cool. Pour paraffin ½″ deep into muffin cups. Insert a wick (1½″ long) so it comes out on the side. Just before paraffin hardens, press a pine cone into the top. Allow to harden. Dip bottom of muffin tins into hot water to loosen, and remove fire starters.

Melt a small amount of paraffin in a small pan, following the above melting procedure. Tint the wax red or green by melting a crayon into it. Cool slightly. Dip the bottom of each fire starter into the colored paraffin. Dry on waxed paper.

To use, place a fire starter under kindling and light the wick.

Holiday Goose

A weathered goose decoy, shiny magnolia leaves and holly, polished red and yellow apples, and a scattering of chestnuts become a striking centerpiece and demonstrate again how Christmas can inspire us—as other seasons fail to do—to "dress" a treasured object and bring it into the limelight.

Christmas Potpourri

The nostalgic flavor of this simple holiday arrangement heightens the spirit of today's Christmas and conjures memories of those past. The timeworn St. Nicholas, dressed in his bishop's robe as the Europeans imagine him and appearing much thinner than the round and jolly St. Nick we know, stands amidst a chocolate pot and mugs, wooden blocks, a tiny tree with antique glass ornaments, and other things of old.

Christmas Bazaar

The crisp coolness of fall brings a sense of anticipation for the season that lies ahead, and our thoughts turn to plans for Christmas. Quiet moments spent now making gifts and decorations for the holidays will give you free time to spend with the family later on.

Whether you are handiest with a needle, paint and paper, or simply puttering around in the kitchen, there is a project for you in our Christmas Bazaar of ideas. If your favorite needlecraft is smocking, applique, patchwork, or bargello, you will find a new design here. Bread dough can be quickly and easily baked into Christmas ornaments, and St. Nick himself can be cut from wood. To make the Eyelet Wreaths and Angel Pocket, you need no special skills—just enthusiasm and simple materials. If, like most of us, you save bits of ribbon and laces all year long, bring them out and put them to work by creating one-of-a-kind gifts: spicy pomanders, Victorian wraps, clothespin dolls.

Children love to get in on the fun of Christmas, and our Children's Workshop is full of suggestions for things that just fit their busy little hands. There is a Gumdrop Wreath for their door or for a gift. A Pecan Wreath that becomes a centerpiece for the family table can truly make a child proud to share his handiwork with others. There are Sugarplum Lollipops and Raffia Wreaths to use as ornaments or as easy and inexpensive gifts for friends. Make a special paper or a package accent from our Wraps designs.

Get started now—while you have the time to enjoy creating gifts and decorations—so that, this year, you are ready to relax and enjoy the holiday with the people you love.

Easy Holiday Crafts

Partridges & Pears

Partridges and pears bring the traditional melody to a matching tree skirt, ornaments, and stockings—all so simple to make and so inviting in your home this season.

TREE SKIRT

MATERIALS (for 42″-diameter tree skirt):
   patterns on pages 138-139
   3⅓ yards (45″-wide) green broadcloth
   9″ × 11″ felt squares: 2 yellow, 2 white, 1
      light green
   embroidery floss: 1 dark green, 1 yellow
   1 spool transparent thread
   1 spool green sewing thread
   3 (2½-yard) packages white bias corded
      piping
   4 yards white eyelet ruffle
   42″ × 42″ square of polyester quilt
      batting
   1⅓ yards green satin ribbon

Enlarge the pattern for the skirt panel to correct size. Cut 16 pieces from green broadcloth: 8 for the top and 8 for the lining. From felt, cut the 4 yellow pears, 4 white birds and wings, and 4 sets of light green leaves and stems.

Position the felt cutouts on the broadcloth. Pin or baste to hold them in place. Using a zigzag stitch and transparent thread, sew around all the pieces. Accent birds' wings with yellow floss and a running stitch around the edges. Use dark green floss to make one French knot for the eye.

Using a zipper foot and a long stitch, baste the bias piping along both long sides of one bird panel, leaving a ⅜″ seam allowance. Lay one pear panel on the bird panel, right sides together, and sew one side together along basting line.

Baste the piping to the other long side of the pear panel. Continue to alternate panels and piping in this manner. On the last panel, sew the piping to the remaining long side but do not sew the circle together.

Place eyelet ruffle around circle, right sides down. Using a ⅜″ seam and a zipper foot, sew eyelet around scalloped edges of circle.

Sew lining panels together. Do not join the circle. Press seams open.

Place the lining on batting, and cut the batting to fit. Pin the batting to the back side of the lining. Pin the skirt top to lining, right sides together. Using a zipper foot, sew through all thicknesses. Leave an opening in one end panel for turning. Trim seams. Clip curves and scallops. Turn skirt through opening, and steam press. Baste opening closed.

Cut 6 (8″-long) pieces of ribbon; position 3 on each back panel edge and sew in place. These are to be tied together to secure the skirt around the tree.

ORNAMENTS

MATERIALS:
   patterns on pages 138-139
   9″ × 11″ felt squares in white, yellow,
      light green
   green ribbon
   transparent thread
   batting
   embroidery floss in yellow and dark
      green

Bird: For each ornament, cut 2 white felt birds, 2 wings and 1 (6″-long) piece of green ribbon. For eyes, embroider dark green French knots on both sides of the bird. Fold the ribbon in half. Pin between the felt pieces at head of bird. Sew the

edges of the bird together by hand or by machine with transparent thread. Stop sewing about 2″ before completing the outline and stuff slightly with batting or cotton. Complete the seam. Join the wings to the body with yellow floss and the outline stitch. Allow the wing tips to hang freely from the body to give dimension, but continue outline stitch around wings.

Pear: Cut 2 yellow felt pears, 1 leaf, and 1 (6″-long) piece of ribbon for each ornament. Fold the ribbon in half. Pin the ribbon at top of pear in place of the stem. Pin the leaf between the felt pieces to one side of the ribbon. Sew the edges and stuff as for the bird ornament.

continued

STOCKINGS

MATERIALS (for 2 stockings):
  patterns on pages 138-139
  1 yard (36"- or 45"-wide) green
    broadcloth
  1 yard white flannel
  polyester batting
  transparent thread
  embroidery floss: 1 strand dark green, 1
    strand yellow
  18" white eyelet ruffling
  18" white bias corded piping
  12" green satin ribbon
  9" × 11" felt squares: 1 white, 1 yellow, 1
    light green

Enlarge the stocking pattern on page 138 to full size.

For each stocking, cut 2 stocking pieces from broadcloth, 2 from flannel, and 2 from batting. Cut 2 stocking cuffs and 2 cuff linings.

For the partridge stocking, cut 4 birds and 4 wings from white felt.

For the pear stocking, cut 4 pears from yellow felt. Cut 4 leaves and 4 stems from green felt.

Position the pears on one set of cuffs and the birds on the other. Appliqué the felt cutouts to the cuffs, using a zigzag stitch and transparent thread. Accent the birds with dark green French knots for eyes and yellow running stitches around the wings. With right sides together, sew front and back seams of cuff, using a ⅜" seam. Press.

Using a zipper foot and a long stitch, baste the eyelet ruffle ⅜" from the lower edge of the cuff with birds. With the zipper foot and a long stitch, baste piping on the cuff with pears. With right sides together, sew front and back seams of cuff lining. Press.

Place cuff and lining with right sides together, and sew through both thicknesses along the eyelet or piping basting lines. Trim. Turn and press. Pin batting to the wrong side of the stocking pieces. Place stockings with right sides together, and sew through all thicknesses, using a ⅝" seam. Trim and clip curves. Turn and press.

Sew flannel lining seams right sides together. Do not turn the flannel. Turn under ¾" along the top edge. Press.

Slide the stocking into the cuff, matching top edges of cuff and stocking. Sew cuff to stocking, allowing a 1" seam. Turn the raw edges to inside along seam line. Cut 1 piece of ribbon 6" long. Fold to make a loop. Sew just inside the back seam.

Slip the flannel lining into the stocking. Pin the lining to the stocking ¼" above the seam that joins cuff to the stocking. Whipstitch in place.

Christmas Album

Where is the photograph of the children with Santa that was made two years ago? And how about that favorite shot of Granddad helping to set up the train? Here is a special album for all your Christmas keepsake photographs.

MATERIALS:
   pattern on page 143
   ⅔ yard red calico
   8¼″ × 4½″ muslin for embroidery
   DMC embroidery floss, (#666 red)
   1 yard ¼″-wide lace
   1 yard ⅜″-wide braid
   transparent thread
   9″ × 11″ felt squares: 1 green, 1 red
   12½″ × 21½″ polyester batting
   photo album (11½″ × 10″)

From calico, cut 2 pieces that are 12½″ × 9″ and 2 pieces that are 12½″ × 21½″. Transfer the lettering from page 143 to muslin. Embroider the word *Christmas* in satin stitches. Embroider other words with outline stitch. Run a second row of outline stitch beside the first as indicated by the embroidery pattern.

Center the embroidered muslin on one end of one 12½″ × 21½″ piece of calico with the bottom edge of muslin 3½″ from one 12½″-long bottom edge of the calico. Pin in place. Position lace around edges of muslin. Sew with transparent thread and zigzag stitch, catching both the muslin and the lace with the same stitches. Position gold braid over the first zigzag stitches. Zigzag over braid.

Cut 6 green felt holly leaves and 5 red felt berries. Position in the corners of the embroidered muslin. Zigzag around the leaves, and tack the centers of the berries in place with transparent thread.

Turn under ¼″ twice along one long side of both 12½″ × 9″ pieces of calico.

Lay the embroidered cover right side up on the piece of batting. Place smaller pieces of calico right side down on cover, matching outside edges

and having finished edges of smaller pieces toward center. Lay the remaining large piece of calico right side down over all. Pin around all edges. Sew through all thicknesses (½″ seam allowance), leaving an opening in one side for turning. Trim seams and corners. Turn and press. Slipstitch opening closed. Slip album cover into the pockets.

Clothespin Dolls

Parade these soldiers and their ladies on a table laden with small packages or use them to trim your tree. Clothespin dolls are fun to make and can be dressed in a myriad of ways—begin a tradition by making new dolls each Christmas.

MATERIALS:
   clothespins
   acrylic paints in red and blue
   cardboard
   white household glue
For each soldier:
   popsicle stick
   1″ pompom for hat
   ¾″ (⅜″-wide) fancy braid for hat
   10″ (⅛″-wide) gold braid
   2½″ (¼″-wide) gold braid
For each lady:
   pipe cleaner
   9″ brown yarn for hair
   3″ (1″-wide) blue ribbon
   5½″ (1¼″-wide) lace
   7″ (3¼″-wide) blue eyelet
   tiny straw or other dried flowers

For soldier: Paint the clothespin blue to the notch and red from the end of the notch to the "neck." Cut a 1¾″ length from each end of a popsicle stick. Paint both sides red. Paint a 1½″ square of cardboard blue. With a toothpick that has a very fine end, draw a face with black acrylic paint; it is a good idea to practice on a scrap of paper to make the features tiny enough.

Glue on a pompom hat. Glue the fancy braid to the hat. Glue the clothespin to the cardboard.

Glue the ⅛″-wide braid along the side of trouser. Wrap ⅛″-wide braid around neck and across the chest. Glue in place. Wrap the ¼″-wide braid around the waist, covering raw ends of trouser strips and chest braid and where the blue and red paint meet. Glue the popsicle stick arms into place.

For lady: Paint facial features. Glue doll to a 1½″ square of cardboard. Glue 4 (2¼″-long) strands of yarn across top of head.

For arms, cut a pipe cleaner in half. Turn back a "hand" at one end of each piece. Roll other ends into circles until "arms" are about 1½″ long. Glue rolled ends to sides of clothespin.

Cut a small hole in the center of the length of ribbon and slip over head of doll. Pull ends of ribbon straight down at front and back, and glue. Loosely wrap the strip of lace to form a shawl. Hold in place with a rubber band. Sew together ends of wide eyelet for skirt. Turn seam to inside. Turn inside the raw edge of top of eyelet, and run a gathering thread (by hand) around top of skirt. Put the skirt on doll, over ends of ribbon and shawl lace. Pull gathering thread to fit waist, and tack to hold gathers and shawl in place.

Pull arms into a pleasing position. Tuck a few straw flowers into the bend of the lady's hand.

The Pungence of Pomanders

Spice-scented fruits fill the air with a pungent holiday fragrance. They make welcome gifts and are so simple that even older children can join in the fun. Pomanders can be restored to their original fragrance and used for many years.

MATERIALS:

nut pick, knitting needle, or similar pointed utensil
oranges, pears, lemons, or similar fruit
whole cloves (1 large can for each ball)
powdered cinnamon (1 tablespoon for each ball, or 2 tablespoons for each ball if orris root is not used)
powdered orris root, if available (1 tablespoon for each ball)
decorative trimmings: ribbons, laces

Ideally, your pomanders should be made at least six weeks before Christmas to allow time for natural drying; however, they can be made at the last minute and then dried in the oven.

Use your pointed utensil to pierce the skin to avoid breaking the clove tops. Stick the whole cloves into the fruit rind. Cloves need not be set in rows or in any pattern, but if you wish to tie a ribbon around the pomander, you should leave an empty channel the width of the ribbon as you press cloves into the fruit.

Mix the orris root and cinnamon in a bowl (use cinnamon alone if the orris root is unavailable). Roll the clove-covered fruit in the spice mixture until it is completely covered. Next, wrap the pomander loosely in tissue paper and place it in a dry, warm drawer, cupboard, or closet for four to six weeks. Inspect the pomanders from time to time. If the fruits are drying too fast, they may shrivel; too slowly, they may mildew. The drying process may be speeded up by partially drying the pomanders in a slow (200°F.) oven for several hours and then allowing them to continue drying as above in the time remaining until they are needed.

When the pomanders are dry, shake off the excess powder. Decorate with ribbons, lace, greenery, or dried flowers.

The fragrance of the pomanders can be restored and they can be used from year to year. To do this, remove the trimmings. Then simply boil the pomanders. Roll the fruit again in the cinnamon/orris root mixture as described above and dry in a slow oven overnight.

Christmas Lace

Crisp, white eyelet is combined with shiny red berries and velvet ribbon in these easy-to-make wreaths. No special skills are needed for this project—and the attractive wreaths can be used to cheer a window or to set the mood on your holiday table.

WINDOW WREATH

MATERIALS:
    10″-diameter Styrofoam® plate
    2 yards (¼″-wide) red velvet ribbon
    5¼ yards (1½″-wide) eyelet
    4 yards florist's wire
    red felt for a 10″-diameter circle
    fabric glue
    scotch tape
    2 or 3 clusters of red berries
    stapler

Cut a 4″-diameter hole in center of plate.

Cut an 8″-long piece of ribbon. Form a loop and staple the ends 1″ from edge of plate. Cut eyelet into 4 lengths: 2 yards, 1½ yards, 1 yard, and ¾ yard. Cut wire into 4 pieces: 33″, 26″, 20″, and 14″. Run the longest piece of wire through casing of the 2-yard section of eyelet. Gather to form a circle with a 9″ diameter. Twist wire to close. Gather the 1½-yard piece of eyelet to a 7″-diameter circle, 1 yard to a 5″-diameter circle, and ¾ yard to a 3″-diameter circle. Place eyelet circles on bottom of plate. Glue in place, beginning with largest circle.

Push berry stems through eyelet and plate along bottom of hole. Tape stems on wrong side of plate.

Notch ends of remaining ribbon and form a bow. Wire center of bow. Twist ends of wire at back and push through plate under berries. Tape on wrong side of plate.

Cut 10″-diameter circle of red felt. Cut a 4″-diameter hole in center. Put glue around outer edge of felt and inside edge of hole. Press on back of wreath.

EYELET TREE ORNAMENTS

MATERIALS (for 1 ornament):
   10″ florist's wire
   10″ eyelet (use various widths and
      patterns)
   fabric glue
   10″ (¼″-wide) satin ribbon
   fishing line or ornament hangers

Run the piece of wire through the casing of the eyelet. Gather the eyelet onto the wire, and pull the wire together to form the wreath. The size of the center of the wreath may vary. Twist the wire together and cut it. Make a small bow of ribbon, and glue that to the wreath. Use fishing line or a regular Christmas hanger to loop through the eyelet for hanging.

*Note:*To order a set of four eyelet tree ornaments, send a check or money order for $5.00 (plus $.75 for postage and handling) to American Sampler, 2106 Flowerwood Drive, Birmingham, Alabama 35244. Alabama residents add $.30 tax.

EYELET CENTERPIECE

MATERIALS:
   10″-diameter Styrofoam® plate
   5¼ yards (1½″-wide) eyelet
   4 yards florist's wire
   8 to 10 bunches red berries
   fabric glue
   scotch tape
   red felt for a 10″-diameter circle
   red candle

Cut a hole 3″ in diameter in the center of the plate.

To make the 4 graduated eyelet circles, cut the eyelet into 4 lengths: 2 yards, 1½ yards, 1 yard, and ¾ yard.

Cut the wire into 4 pieces: 33″, 26″, 20″, and 14″. Run the longest piece of wire through the casing of the 2-yard section of eyelet. Gather the eyelet onto the wire to form a circle with a 9″ diameter.

Twist the wire to close. Follow the same procedure with the 1½-yard piece of eyelet and gather to a 7″-diameter circle. Gather 1 yard of eyelet to a 5″-diameter circle and the ¾ yard to a 3″-diameter circle.

Turn the plate bottom side up. Place the eyelet circles on the plate. Make any final adjustments in size before cutting off excess wire.

Glue eyelet circles in place with fabric glue, beginning with the largest circle and ending with the smallest.

Push stems of berry clusters through the eyelet and into the plate to form a circle of berries around the hole in the plate. Tape the stems of the berries on the wrong side of the plate to secure.

Cut a circle of felt that is 10″ in diameter. Attach the felt to the underside of the plate by glueing the outer edge of felt and pressing to plate.

Place candle in center hole.

Holly Place Mats

Set a holiday table with cheery red place mats accented with a cross-stitched holly motif and clever holly leaf napkin rings. A set of four would make an inexpensive—yet beautiful—gift for friends or family. It's a great bazaar idea too!

MATERIALS (4 mats and 4 napkin rings):
  chart and pattern on page 137
  4 pieces (14-count) cross stitch fabric, 2¾″ × 19″ each
  2 skeins green embroidery floss (DMC #700)
  1 skein red embroidery floss (DMC #666)
  ⅞ yards prequilted red dotted fabric
  5 green (9″ × 11″) felt squares
  transparent sewing thread
  2½ yards (⅜″-wide) red satin ribbon
  red sewing thread
  3 packages wide red bias tape
  4 (½″) red ball buttons

Follow the chart to cross stitch one holly motif in the center of one of the cross-stitch fabric panels. Work 4 motifs on either side of the center, having 25 spaces between the stitches that form the top of the holly leaf. Repeat on all 4 panels.

Cut 4 (19″ × 14½″) pieces of the prequilted red fabric. From each corner, measure 2″ in both directions and draw a line between these points. Cut the corners along the line.

Cut felt into 3¾″-wide strips. Pin the felt to the mats with the bottom edge of the felt strips even with the top edge of the angle at the corners. Piece the felt lengthwise by overlapping felt strips in the center of the mat. Using a zig-zag stitch with transparent thread on top, sew along the long edges of the felt. Trim felt even with mat.

Position the cross-stitched panel over the center of the felt strip. Place satin ribbon over the raw edges at the top and bottom of the cross stitched panel. Pin. Using transparent thread and straight stitch, sew along both edges of each ribbon. Trim excess.

With red thread, sew wide bias tape over all the edges of the mat. Press.

For the holly napkin rings, cut 8 felt holly leaves according to pattern. Cut 4 pieces of ribbon 4¾″ long.

Place 2 felt pieces together. Place ribbon piece along center of the stem and with end of ribbon even with end of holly stem, as shown on the pattern. Topstitch through center of ribbon with transparent thread. Continue stitching to end of leaf. Work the button hole at end of ribbon. Sew the button to the end of stem. Wrap the stem around napkin and button in place.

Jolly St. Nick

Jolly St. Nick stands 18″ high and is made from only three simple pattern pieces. He can be made to sit or stand, and he is sure to add a touch of holiday merriment to your mantel or serve as a welcome host on your entry hall table.

MATERIALS:
   pattern on pages 140-141
   1″ × 12″ × 24″ pine shelving
   5″ dowel (½″ in diameter)
   latex gloss enamel: black, red, white, yellow
   semi-gloss spray varnish
   4 (1″) wire brads

Transfer pattern to wood. Cut around the outlines, using a jigsaw or band saw. Mark the dowel positions. Drill ½″ holes for the dowels. Sand all the edges and surfaces. Transfer features for painting onto wood. Spray a thin coat of varnish over all surfaces and allow to dry completely. This will seal the wood and provide a better surface for applying the enamel. Paint the details as indicated on the pattern pieces. Allow to dry overnight. Spray with another coat of varnish.

Cut 2 (2½″-long) pieces of the dowel. To attach the legs, slide one dowel into the hole on one leg until the end of dowel is flush with outside leg surface. Drill a 1/16″ pilot hole through the top of the leg and the dowel. (This will prevent leg from splitting when inserting nail.) Permanently secure leg to dowel by nailing a 1″ wire brad through the pilot hole.

Slide the dowel through hole in body. All dowels should fit tightly to allow for more controlled movement of Santa. Position the other leg onto the protruding portion of the dowel. There will be some space between the legs and the body to prevent friction. Secure the leg to the dowel as before, using 1/16″ pilot hole and 1″ wire brad. Attach arms, using the same method as was used for the legs. For the best effect, leave one arm higher than the other to add a good balance in appearance. Use touch-up paint over the nail ends.

Cross-Stitched Ornaments

Cross stitch highlights the softness of these winsome Christmas tree ornaments. They are also perfect little "dolls" for Santa to tuck into a child's stocking.

MATERIALS:
  charts on pages 144-145
For each ornament:
  8″ × 6½″ piece of 14-count Aida cloth (ivory for angel, and soldier; white for panda)
  8″ × 6½″ piece of medium-weight linen or muslin for backing
  4″ red cord
  polyester fiberfill
  #24 tapestry needle

For angel:
  DMC floss in golden yellow (725), light blue (799), yellow (444), flesh (945), pink (3326), light green (703), dark green (904), red (817)

For panda:
  DMC floss in white, black (310), light green (703), dark green (904), red (817), light blue (799)
For soldier:
  DMC floss in red (666), royal blue (792), golden yellow (725), white, medium brown (434), flesh (951), black (310)

Stitch designs on the center of each piece of Aida cloth according to the charts, using 2 strands of floss. Follow backstitching instructions given on each chart.

Press the wrong side of the stitched designs, using a damp press cloth.

With a pencil, lightly sketch cutting lines ½″ from the edge of the cross stitching on all sides of ornaments. See photograph for general outline of the ornaments. Place ornament front on top of backing and cut both pieces together, following pencil lines.

Fold the 4″-long piece of cord in half to form a loop. Place the raw edges of the loop on the right side of the Aida at the top of the ornament, with the loop hanging down into the ornament. Pin in place.

Place embroidered piece and backing right sides together, and carefully machine stitch with a ¼″ seam allowance. Leave an opening at the bottom for turning. Clip seams and carefully turn to right side. Press both sides, using a damp press cloth.

Lightly stuff with polyester. Slipstitch opening closed.

Angel Pocket

A pair of smiling angels can fly over an inside door or window to carry greenery, as shown here, or to catch Christmas greeting cards in their pocket. (The angels might even consent to have their pocket filled with holiday candy for the sweet tooth in your family.)

MATERIALS:
   pattern on pages 142-143
   felt in red, flesh pink, rose, white, blue,
      purple, lilac, and yellow
   red embroidery floss
   sequins, some decorative
   beads
   household glue
   suit-weight fusible interfacing
   polyester fiberfill
   2 small plastic loops

Trace the pattern given on page 142. Be sure to make a one-piece pattern that will be the base of the whole angel, including wings and body (the darkest lines on the pattern).

Cut felt in the following number of pieces and colors: 4 whole angel shapes from white, 2 pockets from red, 2 pockets from interfacing, 2 robes from blue, 2 sleeves and 2 sleeve parts from lilac, 2 sleeve trims from purple, 2 hair shapes from yellow, 2 faces from flesh pink, 2 hands from flesh pink, 4 cheeks from rose.

As you make the angels, reverse each pattern piece so you make one angel a mirror image of the other.

On each of the faces, embroider a mouth with red thread; add a bead for nose, sequins for eyes, and the rosy cheeks. Sew rows of sequins around the neck and hem of the gowns. Sew halos of sequins on hair. Sew large decorative sequins on wings. Glue two of the whole angel shapes together, leaving an opening at bottom for stuffing.

Glue robe, face, hair, and sleeve piece (that goes behind pocket) in position on angels. Allow to dry. Stuff lightly with fiberfill, and whipstitch together.

Attach fusible interfacing to the inside of both pocket pieces, following manufacturer's instructions. Sew sequins and beads to one pocket piece. Glue front to back around the edges, leaving the top open for inserting cards or greenery.

Glue pocket to angels, checking the photograph for placement.

Sew sequins to sleeve trim, and glue trim to sleeves. Place sleeves on angels to check placement for hands. Slip hands beneath the edges of sleeves, and glue hands in place. Glue sleeves into place. Allow to dry thoroughly.

Tack plastic loop behind each angel's head to form hangers.

Needlepoint Sparklers

Yesterday's Christmases sparkle in our memories like the star of long ago. The time-honored craft of needlepoint makes use of modern metallic thread that will catch that star today in ornaments for your tree, as you create hand-stitched remembrances to keep for years to come.

MATERIALS (for 1 star):
   2 (5"-square) pieces of #14 interlock needlepoint canvas
   clear nail polish or masking tape
   tapestry needle
   1 skein each in 3 graduated shades of 1 color of #3 or #5 perle cotton or 6-ply embroidery floss
   gold or silver metallic yarn (amount varies with thickness)

Tape the edges of the canvas or stiffen with clear nail polish. Use 2 strands of floss, 2 strands of #5 perle cotton, or 1 strand of #3 perle. Use the number of strands of metallic yarn that best covers the canvas.

Follow the chart given here to make two star shapes, a front and a back for each star. Begin with the darkest shade of thread and use a bargello stitch.

To begin the design, find the center hole of your canvas. Work a stitch that comes up 4 threads from the right of center and goes down into the center. Work a stitch that comes up 4 threads left of center and goes into the center. Work stitches over 4 threads from above and below the center hole. Work 4 diagonal stitches, each over 3 intersections, also going into the center hole.

The following rows continue the pattern of bargello stitches taken over 4 threads for straight stitches and over 3 intersections for diagonal stitches. To lessen fraying of yarn, work the bargello stitch so that it comes up in an empty hole and goes down into a filled hole.

To duplicate the patterns of colors shown in the photograph, work the second row with metallic yarn, a third row with the medium shade of colored thread, a fourth row with metallic yarn, a fifth row with the lightest shade of colored thread and a sixth row with metallic yarn.

Note: Work as many or few rows as you wish, following the pattern. The pattern will also apply to larger or smaller canvas; adjust thread size or number of threads.

To assemble the ornaments, cut the canvas 2 rows beyond the worked area. Brush the edges with clear nail polish and allow to dry. Turn under the edges, place the star shapes back to back, and pin securely at each point. Whipstitch together with the lightest shade of colored thread, matching threads of canvas as you go. Attach a loop of thread for hanging.

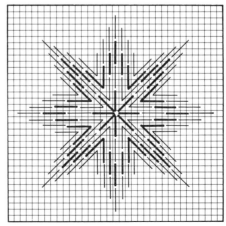

Smocked Sherbets

Scrumptious colors and feminine ruffles blend in these elegant stockings. The soft pastel shades and the glimmering moiré, topped off with a dollop of crisp white eyelet, are just right for the special little girl in your life.

MATERIALS:
chart and pattern on page 144
⅔ yard moiré
20″ (5″-wide) eyelet
sewing thread to match moiré
embroidery floss to match moiré
16″ (½″-wide) white satin ribbon

Transfer dots to eyelet, on wrong side, using a disappearing marking pen. With a heavyweight thread in a color that contrasts with the eyelet, gather the eyelet by running the needle through each dot in each row. Gather the eyelet along the threads, tying off the loose ends so that the gathered eyelet is ½″ smaller than the width of stocking top.

Smock the eyelet as shown on the chart, using 3 strands of the embroidery floss.

Enlarge the stocking pattern shown on page 144 to full size. Cut 2 stocking shapes from moiré.

Machine baste the smocked piece to the front of stocking, stitching along the top and sides of the eyelet. Cut a 7″-long bias strip of moiré. Place right sides together, and sew along top of stocking front and eyelet. Turn to the inside to form a narrow bias binding. Stitch.

Hem the back of the stocking by folding top down ¼″, folding under again 1½″, and stitching in place.

Sew stocking front to stocking back with a French seam. Press.

Cut a 4″ long piece of ribbon and fold into a loop for hanging. Attach to inside of stocking at the back seam. Make a bow of the remaining ribbon and tack to outside of stocking at back seam.

Baker's Ornaments

For an easy, penny-wise craft, you needn't look farther than your kitchen cupboard. With a few homely ingredients, you can stir up a marvelous mixture that children and adults alike will enjoy molding into Christmas ornaments.

MATERIALS:
    patterns on page 134
    baker's clay (recipe below)
    felt tip pen
    acorns or other trim
    food coloring
    spray acrylic
    narrow ribbon in red, gold, green

Baker's clay: Combine 4 cups all-purpose flour with 1 cup salt; add 1½ cups water and mix. Turn out mixture on a foil-covered cookie sheet, and knead to a putty-like consistency (about 10 minutes). Keep the clay you are not using wrapped in plastic, as it dries out quickly.

Wreath ornament: Roll dough to ⅜" thickness. Cut out wreath shape with outer circle about 6" in diameter and a 3"-diameter hole in center. Using top of felt-tip pen, press holes all around outer edge and one hole at top near inner edge. Press acorns around wreath. Shape leaves by hand (using a toothpick to "etch" the veins), and press onto wreath, half covering the acorns. (Moisten leaves to make them "stick.") Roll tiny

berries from dough and add to leaf clusters. Bake in 350°F. oven for 45 minutes or until brown; cool. Paint leaves and berries with diluted food coloring. Seal with acrylic spray. Weave with ribbon, leaving extra at ends for bow. Pull ribbon through hole at inside edge of top, and tie bow.

Heart ornaments: Trace patterns (page 134) and cut out. Roll dough to a ⅜" thickness. Place paper patterns on dough and mark around edge by dotting with a toothpick. Carefully cut out shapes with a knife. Punch holes for ribbon weaving as desired. Join shapes by moistening with water and pressing together (the heart, star, flower, and bird ornament) or leave shapes unjoined (the heart and flower ornament). Bake, cool, and seal as above. Weave with ribbon and tie.

Note: To hang, punch a hole near top of piece as you fashion it. When the ornament is finished, add a ribbon, silk cord, or aluminum wire (salt content may corrode some metal hangers).

Sweet Gum Garland

Nature lovers will delight in this garland that is just the right accent wherever a natural and unsophisticated—but very festive—decoration is desired. Free for the gathering, the sweet gum balls can be collected by the family in a day of outdoor fun. Use an electric drill to make the holes through the balls and string the balls onto fishing line with a large needle.

Patchwork Wreaths

Pieced from only 3 simple pattern pieces, this wreath can have many variations through the fabrics you choose, and it will last for years.

MATERIALS:
>   **pattern on page 137**
>   **½ yard (45″-wide) fabric**
>   **¼ yard each of 2 different fabrics**
>   **polyester fiberfill**
>   **2 yards ribbon**

Using the full-size patterns, cut 3 templates. Choose the fabric for each template: all the rectangles should be from one fabric, all the hexagons from a second fabric, and all the diamonds from a third. The hexagons require more fabric (½ yard). Trace around the template on the wrong side of your fabric. Add ¼″ seam allowances, and cut 16 pieces by each template (8 for front of wreath, 8 for back).

Right sides together, sew side A of one rectangle to side A of one hexagon. Press open. Repeat to join all 16 rectangles and hexagons.

Right sides together, place diamond so that point A matches the seam between the rectangle and hexagon and one side of diamond aligns with the long side of rectangle. Starting at point A, sew along side of rectangle; then sew from point A along side of hexagon. Press seam open.

Attach another diamond to the other side of the rectangle-hexagon piece in the same manner. Continue adding a rectangle-hexagon and then a diamond until 8 diamonds, 8 hexagons, and 8 rectangles have been used. Join to form a circle. Press seams open. This is the front of wreath.

Repeat above steps to make back of wreath.

Place front and back with right sides together. Line up the pieces—hexagon to hexagon, diamond to diamond, rectangle to rectangle, with seams meeting at edges. Pin or baste. Stitch outside edge of wreath, making certain seams and pieces match. Leave inside circle open.

Turn wreath right side out. Press ¼″ seam allowance under all around the inside. Stuff with fiberfill. Pin seam together, and whipstitch closed.

Make a bow and pin to front of wreath.

Children's Workshop

Gumdrop Wreath

Make this yummy wreath just for the fun of it, and don't be surprised if you find bits of it missing during the holidays.

MATERIALS:
   4 (9-ounce) packages soft gumdrops
   12-inch Styrofoam® wreath
   round wooden toothpicks
   fabric or ribbon bow
   florist's pick

Sort the gumdrops by color to help you remember to use all colors all around the wreath.

Wrap a wire to make a loop for hanging.

Break toothpicks in half. Push one end of the half of toothpick into the Styrofoam® wreath. Press a gumdrop on the pick. Add more gumdrops. Place the gumdrops so close together that they touch. Cover wreath with gumdrops.

Wrap the wire of the florist's pick around the bow. Push the pick into the wreath.

Ribbons & Raffia

Tiny raffia wreaths are inexpensive to make and are wonderful ornaments or package embellishments. Children will enjoy making them and using their imagination to decorate with bits of ribbon and dried flowers.

MATERIALS:
   raffia
   narrow ribbon
   dried flowers
   holly leaves and berries

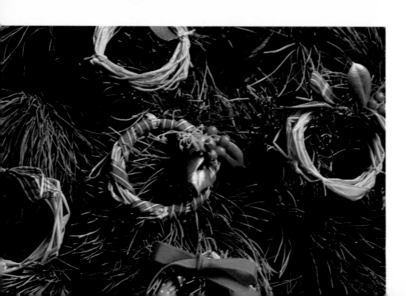

Cut several pieces of raffia (2″ long) for ties. Tie several lengths of raffia together to form one long strand. Loop the raffia round and round until a wreath is formed. To secure the wreath in its circular form, tie the 2″ pieces around the wreath in 3 or 4 places. Trim. Tie a bow to each wreath and tuck in a sprig of holly or small dried flowers.

Holiday Painter's Pants

Whether jumping or climbing or sitting on Santa's knee, a child is perfectly dressed for the season when he is wearing clothes that are hand-painted with cheery Christmas designs. Simple outlines and just a few bright colors of paint transform plain overalls (or even nearly-outgrown clothes) into holiday fashions.

Older children can handle the project from start to finish; younger ones will probably need to let Mom, Dad, or Big Brother do most of the actual painting. Tots will enjoy pointing out just where the candy canes, Santas, or their name should go. They'll be just as thrilled with the results as if they had done it all by themselves!

MATERIALS:
  acrylic fabric paints
  overalls

Cover the kitchen table with newspapers or a plastic dropcloth; then stretch out the garment so that it lies flat. Decide on the placement of the designs and lightly draw them with a pencil.

Use acrylic fabric paints to give the best coverage. (Other acrylic paints, such as artist's colors that come in tubes, may also be used.) Paint any large areas of color first; then add details. Allow to dry completely, and press on the wrong side with a warm iron to set the design. As with any painted garment, the overalls should only be washed by hand.

Tiny Tabletop Tree

Use brightly colored squares of tissue to make this festive paper tree. Mom may need to mark and cut the squares, but the fun of making and decorating the tree is just for the kids.

MATERIALS:
   colored tissue paper
   12"-high Styrofoam® cone
   white household glue
   brush for applying glue
   pencil with an eraser

Cut out 3" squares of green tissue paper. Beginning at the top of the tree, brush glue on a small section of the Styrofoam® cone. Set eraser of pencil in the center of a tissue paper square (A). Pull the square of tissue around the end of the pencil (B). Poke the square onto the cone and slip the pencil out. Repeat until the section that is covered with glue is completely filled. (Place these tissue squares close together so tree will be fluffy.) Spread glue on another section and fill with tissue. Continue doing this until the entire cone is covered.

Cut out 2" squares of tissue paper of various colors. Use these to make "ornaments" for the tree. After pulling the tissue around the end of the pencil, dip tissue in small amount of glue. Gently poke tissue into tree. Repeat until tree is decorated.

To make the garland, cut a long strip of red tissue. Hold the ends of the strip between your fingers and gently twist. Wrap the garland around and around the tree. Top the tree with a "star" that is a cluster of bright yellow tissue.

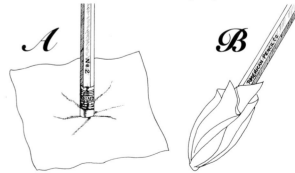

68

Ring around the Candle

Even young children can easily make this pretty wreath, and their little eyes will light up with pride when they see it used as a candle ring or hung on the wall. A light spray of varnish (added by Mother) lends shine and durability.

MATERIALS:
  corrugated cardboard
  pecans
  white glue
  spray varnish (optional)
  candle (optional)
  ribbon

Draw a wreath shape on the cardboard. For the small inside circle, use either a large glass or the candle itself as a guide. For the larger outside circle, use a plate approximately 10″ in diameter. Cut out the wreath shape.

Place a small amount of glue on the bottom of each pecan, and arrange the nuts on the cardboard base. Avoid letting the nuts extend over the edge of the inside circle because this circle must be big enough to hold the candle. Complete the bottom layer. Then add more nuts to form a pleasing arrangement. Allow to dry overnight.

Ask Mother to help spray the wreath with several light coats of varnish. When it is dry, add a ribbon bow and tuck in bits of greenery.

Sugarplum Lollipops

Make these perky "sugarplums" to hang on your tree, to decorate a pretty package, or to give to all of your friends.

MATERIALS:
  squares of felt in bright colors
  popsicle sticks
  scraps of rickrack, colored string, and ribbons
  plastic eyes for faces
  white household glue

Draw around a cup or similar round object to make 2 circles on your felt. Cut out the circles.

Glue the popsicle stick to one circle.

Cut a string to make a loop for hanging. Loop the string and put the ends on the circle. Glue the front circle to the back, keeping the ends of the loop between the circles.

Decorate the lollipops with presents or flowers or trees from felt. Glue on eyes and add a mouth to make a face. Trim with rickrack, string, or narrow ribbons.

Wraps

Angels, Soldiers & Santas

The lively Santas, angels, and soldiers that brighten these tissue-wrapped gifts are so cute that they can be used to decorate your tree as well as your packages. Cut from felt, these figures are inexpensive to make and easy to assemble.

MATERIALS:
    patterns on page 143
    paper for tracing patterns
    white glue
    black razor-point marker
  For Santa:
    pink, red, black, and white felt
    1″ red ball fringe
    ½″ white ball fringe
  For angel:
    pink, gold, and white felt
    1″-wide white fringe
  For soldier:
    pink, blue, black, and gold felt
    1″ blue ball fringe
    ½″ black ball fringe

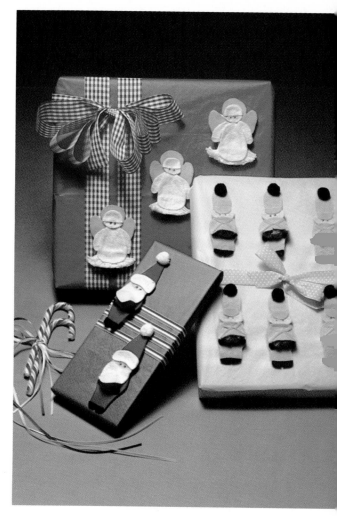

For Santa: Trace and cut out pattern pieces for Santa's body, hat brim, face, beard, hands, and shoes. Draw around pattern pieces on felt and cut out. Glue the 1″ red ball fringe on Santa's stomach. Glue on (in this order) face, hat brim, beard, hands, and shoes. Glue the ½″ white ball fringe on hat. Make eyes with marker.

For angel: Trace and cut out pattern pieces for the angel's body, dress, arms, face, hair, and shoes. Draw around pattern pieces on felt and cut out. Glue 1″-wide white fringe above feet on angel's body. Glue on (in this order) arms, dress, face, hair, hands, and shoes. Make eyes with marker.

For soldier: Trace and cut out pattern pieces for soldier's body, hat bill, face, coat, coat straps, hands, and shoes. Draw around pattern pieces on felt and cut out. Glue 1″ blue ball fringe on soldier's stomach. Glue straps on coat. Glue on (in this order) face, hat bill, coat, hands, and shoes. Glue ½″ black ball fringe on top of hat. Make eyes with marker.

Handprinted Paper

Here is a Christmas wrapping paper that children delight in painting . . . and chances are that Grandmother will carefully save it, cherishing the little hands that made it.

MATERIALS:
   white shelf paper
   tempera paint (red and green)
   large paintbrush

Dress children in smocks or old shirts before starting. Cover the table or floor with lots of newspapers. Then unroll the paper to be painted. Use the tempera paint directly from the jar or, if the mouth of the paint jar is not as wide as the paintbrush, pour some paint into a small dish. Work with only one paint at a time so that colors are not muddied.

   Have the child hold up both of his hands while the parent or older child brushes the paint over the palms. Each time the hands are painted, the child holds his fingers apart and presses down firmly to make a handprint. When enough of one color has been done, then begin on the next. (Tempera paint is non-toxic, but it should be washed off the hands with soap and water. A bit of cleansing cream will remove any traces that remain.)

Victorian Whimsies

These frankly fancy packages are enticingly feminine in shades of soft pink, cream, and silver. One package, wrapped in silver, is over-wrapped with net. Scraps of laces and rich, satiny ribbons are tied gracefully around the packages. Finishing touches include a puff of net, a cluster of dried baby's breath, silver-sprayed holly and deodar cedar cones, dried and pressed flowers, a nosegay from the dimestore, and a silk rose.

Dip-Dyed Paper

An easy way to personalize your Christmas wraps is to color your own tissue paper by dipping it into food coloring. Folds in the paper make the pattern repeats across the sheet.

MATERIALS:
   white tissue paper
   food coloring
   spring clothespins

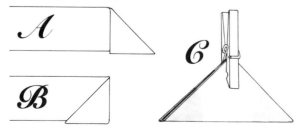

Separate sheets of white tissue paper and fold again along original fold lines. Then fold into triangles as shown (A and B), continuing the folds until the entire length is folded.

Food coloring will stain, so protect cabinets and other surfaces from drips with waxed paper. Place 2 tablespoonfuls of water in a shallow bowl. Add several drops of food coloring to make a very dark solution. (The dyed paper will not be as dark when it dries as when it is wet.) In addition, place a small amount (4 to 5 drops) of food coloring on a piece of waxed paper.

Dip the corners of the folded paper into the solution to penetrate the corners, leaving some of the area between the corners white (C). Then dip the tips of the corners into the undiluted food coloring on the waxed paper to add a darker shade.

Suspend the still folded paper from the clothespin. (A wire through the spring of the clothespin makes a handy hanger.) Allow to dry completely, usually overnight, before unfolding.

Celebrations from the Kitchen

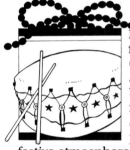

Brisk temperatures, glowing fireplaces, the clean scent of Christmas trees, and the aromas of holiday baking blend together to make a perfect setting for the season's activities. Foods play as important a role in creating a festive atmosphere as do the decorations on the tree. This year we offer you dozens of recipes to add to your time-proven favorites, and you can bake them with confidence since each recipe has been kitchen tested.

We offer the challenge of a new idea for a Gingerbread House. This delectable piece of architecture can be assembled entirely in your kitchen. We provide you with the directions, patterns, and the recipe for the gingerbread. The Gingerbread House is a Christmas decoration you will be proud to display.

Food is always an appropriate and certain-to-please present. With our Party & Gift Ideas section, there is no reason to be concerned about correct sizes or colors; just box up some of our confections and watch those eyes light up.

Just wait until the children hear that you're making Homemade Lollipops or Stained-Glass Windows. You won't have to ask twice for help in pulling the Old-Fashioned Taffy. Our Kids in the Kitchen section offers several recipes that will make your own youngsters want to play a creative part in baking the Christmas treats.

Sweeten the season with Holly Squares, Almond Butter Cake, and Candy-Stuffed Dates. Delight your family with French Lemon Spirals and Swedish Tea Ring. And warm your guests with Hot Mulled Wine and Cranberry Bread. You're sure to be a gracious hostess with foods prepared from our generous assortment of holiday recipes.

Gingerbread House

This Gingerbread House is styled after an old Southern mansion. The front, sides, back, and other parts of the house are cut from gingerbread by the patterns given on page 145. The tall white columns are fashioned of Lifesavers®, and the shingles of the red roof are pieces of gum. The happy Christmas scenes revealed in the windows are piped and filled with Royal Icing on waxed paper that is placed over tracings of our full-size patterns.

The gingerbread house is not difficult to make, but it does take quite some time. It is probably best to plan to make and bake all the pieces one day and assemble them the next.

MATERIALS:
   patterns on pages 145-147
- 2 recipes of Gingerbread (made separately)
- 5 to 7 recipes of Royal Icing (made separately)
- 26" × 22" board for base
- 16 regular marshmallows
   Sifted powdered sugar
- 1 black soft gumdrop
   Assorted candies and decorator sprinkles
   About 17 (7-stick) packages red cinnamon gum
- 2 (.72-ounce) packages white Lifesavers®
   About 16 green soft gumdrops

Cut paper patterns for the pieces of the house to the dimensions given with the patterns. Trace the full-size patterns for the windows, door and porch railing.

Prepare Gingerbread by the following recipe; be sure to follow instructions to make two separate batches instead of doubling the recipe.

Prepare the first batch of Royal Icing when you are ready to make windows. Make additional batches as needed; do not double recipe or make extra batches until ready to use them.

GINGERBREAD

- 2⅓ cups sugar
- ¾ cup honey
- ¼ cup plus 1 tablespoon butter
- ⅓ cup lemon juice
- 1 tablespoon grated lemon rind
- 6¾ cups all-purpose flour
- ¼ cup plus 3½ tablespoons baking powder
- ⅛ teaspoon salt
- 1¾ teaspoons ground ginger
- 1¼ teaspoons ground cinnamon
- ¼ teaspoon ground nutmeg
- ¼ teaspoon ground cloves
- 2 eggs, beaten

Combine sugar, honey, and butter in a 4-quart Dutch oven; bring to a boil, stirring constantly until sugar dissolves. Remove from heat; add the lemon juice and lemon rind, mixing well. Let cool to room temperature.

Combine flour, baking powder, salt, and spices; stir well. Add 2 cups flour mixture and eggs to sugar mixture; mix well. Gradually add remaining flour mixture, mixing well. With lightly floured hands, shape dough into a ball; knead lightly until smooth.

Prepare recipe a second time so you'll have enough dough for a complete house. (Do not double dough initially.) Place one recipe of dough in the refrigerator.

Place three-fourths of second recipe of dough on a greased and floured 16- × 12-inch cookie sheet. Roll dough to about ¼-inch thickness, covering entire cookie sheet. Lightly dust dough with flour and arrange pattern for front of house over dough. Cut around patterns with the tip of

Our gingerbread house will be the centerpiece of any Christmas celebration—it's styled after an old Southern mansion.

Pipe 1 upper left front window.

Pipe 1 upper right front window.

Pipe 1 lower left front window.

Pipe 1 lower right front window.

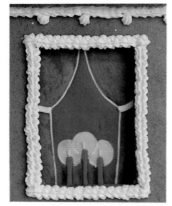

Above: Pipe 2 upper central windows.

Above right: Pipe 2 upper back windows.

Right: Pipe 3 lower back windows.

a knife; cut out windows, door, and slot for porch roof. Remove excess dough; combine with remaining dough and refrigerate.

Bake gingerbread at 325° for 20 minutes or until firm and golden brown. Remove from oven and quickly place patterns over gingerbread. While still warm, cut around outside edges of pattern again on any pieces that rose out of shape, making sure sides of house and roof are straight. Do not trim windows. Carefully slip a spatula under pieces to loosen. Transfer to wire rack to complete cooling. Brush away excess flour.

Repeat procedure with remaining dough, rolling dough to ¼-inch thick. Use pattern for back of house on 1 sheet, cutting windows, cutting a center window instead of door, and omitting porch roof slot. On another cookie sheet, cut 2 roof halves. On each of 2 other cookie sheets, cut 1 house side, 1 porch, 1 inside chimney, and 2 front and back chimneys, cutting and baking each sheet one at a time. On another cookie sheet, cut 2 chimney bases and 2 side chimneys, rolling dough to ⅜-inch thick. Yield: gingerbread for 1 large gingerbread house.

ROYAL ICING

> 3 **large egg whites**
> ½ **teaspoon cream of tartar**
> 1 **(16-ounce) package powdered sugar**
> **Paste food coloring (red, green, gold, blue, lavender, brown, orange, and black)**

Combine egg whites and cream of tartar in a large mixing bowl. Beat at high speed of electric mixer until frothy. Add half of powdered sugar, mixing well. Add remaining sugar, and beat 5 to 7 minutes at high speed. Color small amounts of icing with paste food coloring as needed during decorating. Yield: about 2 cups.

Note: Icing dries very quickly; keep covered at all times with a damp cloth. Do not double recipe. As additional icing is needed, make more batches so icing will be ideal in consistency.

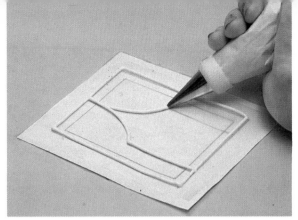

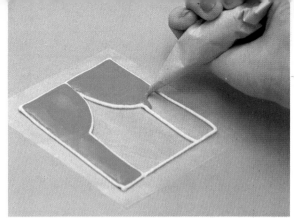

A *Place waxed paper over icing patterns and trace with white icing.*

B *Squeeze flow-in icing inside lines, following numbers on Flow-in Icing Key.*

WINDOWS & OTHER DECORATIONS

For windows, door, and porch railing. Place waxed paper over traced patterns. Prepare a decorating bag with metal decorating tip No. 3. Fill parchment cone half full with white Royal Icing. Pipe icing onto waxed paper to outline figures and inside details (A).

Place a small amount of icing into separate bowls, and color with paste food coloring to make colors specified in Flow-in Icing Key (given with patterns, page 146), mixing small amounts of red and gold paste food coloring with white icing to get a flesh-tone for faces, and a small amount of black with blue coloring for the background color in 2 rooms. Slowly add just enough water to each color to make each a good flowing consistency (hereafter called flow-in icing). Keep icing covered with plastic wrap to prevent it from drying out. If icing separates during the decorating process, stir well before filling decorating bags.

Fill parchment cones about half full of flow-in icing. Snip off small tip of cone and apply icing to cover areas inside outline (B), following numbers on icing patterns and Flow-in Icing Key. Spread icing into corners and hard-to-reach areas with a toothpick.

Work with one color at a time, allowing icing to dry before changing colors. Try to avoid using excess icing as it will spill over into another color area. If the flow-in icing is too watery, it will not dry properly and may run under outline into other color areas. If air bubbles form in icing, use a clean straight pin to remove them.

Prepare additional Royal Icing for shrubbery, trees, wreaths, snowman, and detail on windows that creates a three-dimensional effect (do not dilute this icing). Color small amounts of icing red, gold, green, brown, black, and orange, and leave small amount white.

Using a small amount of white icing, add assorted candies to window scenes as desired. Pipe all detail on window scenes with tip No. 3. Pipe brown strands of hair on children. Pipe red mouths on children, candles in windows, and bows on bear, packages, and in girls' hair. Pipe gold candle flames. Pipe white ruffles around girls' clothing, eyes on teddy bear, and tiebacks and ruffles on curtains. Pipe black eyes on children, and eyes, nose, and mouth on bear. Pipe orange door knob and keyhole.

To make shrubbery, slightly press down 16 regular-sized marshmallows with palm of hand. Place marshmallows on waxed paper and pipe green leaves over top and sides of marshmallows with tip No. 65. Let dry; then peel from paper.

To make trees, make 3 paper cones 6 to 8 inches tall. Stand each cone on waxed paper and pipe a small amount of green icing around base of cones with tip No. 75 or 65. Pipe green leaves on trees with tip No. 75 or 65, working from top to bottom. Let dry; then peel from paper.

To make wreaths, pipe a 1½-inch ring of green icing onto waxed paper with tip No. 14. Pipe leaves on ring with tip No. 65. Pipe red berries on wreath with tip No. 2, and bow with tip No. 101s. Make 4 wreaths. Let dry; then peel from paper.

C *Attach door and windows face-down onto backside of gingerbread, centering over openings.*

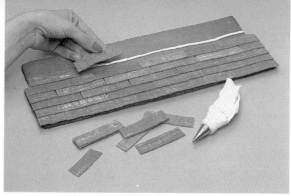

D *Layer strips of gum onto roof, overlapping rows shingle-style.*

To make snowman, place about ⅓ cup white icing in a bowl. Stir in enough powdered sugar to make a soft, moldable consistency. Shape dough into 1½-, 1⅛-, and 1-inch balls, and stick together for snowman with regular consistency icing. Using a sharp knife, slice off a ⅛-inch thick round from a black soft gumdrop. Press in on top and sides of remaining part of gumdrop to condense its size; set condensed part of gumdrop onto slice to form a hat. Insert a wooden pick half-way up through bottom of hat and insert remaining part of pick down head of snowman. Pipe green leaves on hat with tip No. 65. Pipe red band and berries on hat with tip No. 2; pipe red scarf with tip No. 44. Pipe black eyes, mouth, and buttons with tip No. 2. Pipe black arms onto waxed paper with tip No. 2, let dry, and then attach to snowman with white icing. Pipe an orange cone nose onto snowman with tip No. 2. Let snowman dry; then peel from paper.

ASSEMBLING HOUSE

Let window scenes dry completely; then trim away excess waxed paper. Lay front and back of house on wire racks, face down. Pipe a small amount of white icing onto front corners of door and windows with tip No. 3 (C). Center door and windows into respective places on front and back of house. Pipe around inside back edges of door and windows with tip No. 3; smooth excess icing with a knife. Let dry.

Unwrap approximately 90 sticks of gum. Working with 4 or 5 sticks at a time, stack gum on a cutting board and make about 5 unevenly spaced crosswise cuts through gum, cutting to within ⅛-inch of lengthwise edge. Separate sticks of gum, leaving each stick intact. Starting at bottom edge of each roof, pipe a line of icing horizontally across roof and lay strips of gum over line of icing. Add one row at a time, slightly overlapping each row of gum over previous row (D). Let dry.

Pipe icing along the back side edges of front and back of house with tip No. 3. Working with a partner, position front, back, and sides of house in place on a 26- × 22-inch board lined with waxed paper, propping up inside and outside of house with cans or jars (E). Pipe additional icing on inside seams of house for support. Let dry thoroughly.

Pipe icing along all top edges of house with tip No. 3. Position roof on house and hold in place until dry and firm enough to support itself (about 10 minutes). Fold about 5 whole sticks of gum in half lengthwise, and affix at upper seam of roof with icing.

Pipe icing along back edges of side chimney bases and side chimneys. Position onto sides of house, with side chimney centered above chimney base. Prop in place until dry.

Pipe icing along inside edges of remaining chimney pieces. Align pieces against top of side chimney that extends above roof (F).

Pipe molding trim perpendicular to roofline on front and back of house with white icing and tip No. 16, spacing trim ½-inch apart. Pipe horizontal trim all along roofline just above perpendicular trim with white icing and tip No. 16, using a push-and-pull motion of the tip.

Color about ¼ cup regular consistency icing black; dilute with a small amount of water and spread along inside of chimney.

Attach wreaths on front door and on lower back windows with white icing.

Attach floor of front porch in front of door with icing. Cut about 4 sticks of gum crosswise into 7 pieces each. Spread icing evenly over porch and brick the porch with small gum rectangles.

Pipe white molding above door with tip No. 16; pipe white trim around door, all windows, and on all seams and raw edges of house with tip No. 16, using a push-and-pull motion of tip.

Stand 2 drinking straws upright on porch and cut length so porch roof will rest parallel in the slot on front and against top of straws. Thread Lifesavers® onto straws, using about 23 per straw and spreading a small amount of white icing between each. Paste columns in place with icing.

Pipe icing around slot in front for porch roof, and position porch roof in slot and resting on columns (G); pipe a small amount of icing where columns attach with tip No. 3. Let dry.

Pipe trim around porch roof with white icing and tip No. 16. Attach railing on porch roof with white icing and tip No. 3.

Cut about 12 sticks of gum crosswise into 7 pieces each. Spread icing evenly across board for walkway, and brick walkway with small gum rectangles.

Prepare 2 recipes Royal Icing and dilute with water to make a spreading consistency; spread over board to resemble snow (H).

Attach trees, snowman, and piped shrubbery around house with icing; line green gumdrops along walkway as additional shrubbery. Let dry before transporting.

To store the house, cover it loosely with plastic wrap to keep the dust away, and keep it in a cool, dry place.

E Align front, back, and sides of house and prop with small cans or jars until dry; secure with icing.

F Attach chimney tops to roof with icing.

G Position porch roof in slot on front and resting on columns, reinforcing with icing.

H Spread diluted white icing as snow to cover entire platform.

Beverages

HOT MULLED WINE

1½ cups boiling water
½ cup sugar
1 medium lemon, sliced
3 (4-inch) sticks cinnamon
4 whole cloves
½ gallon burgundy or other dry red
    wine
1 orange

Combine first 5 ingredients in a Dutch oven; cook over medium heat until sugar dissolves, stirring occasionally. Add wine and cook over low heat 10 minutes or just until heated. Remove spices and pour into mugs.

Cut a thin strip of orange rind about 10 inches long, using a lemon zester. Tie strip into a bow and spear bow onto tip of a long wooden pick. Insert pick into mug, letting bow rest on rim. Yield: 9½ cups.

HOT SPICED CIDER

2 (4-inch) sticks cinnamon
½ teaspoon whole allspice
½ teaspoon whole cloves
1 quart apple cider
1 quart unsweetened pineapple juice
¼ cup sugar
½ cup lemon juice
1 (25.4-ounce) bottle Sauterne or other
    sweet white wine
    Cinnamon sticks

Tie 2 cinnamon sticks, allspice, and cloves in a cheesecloth bag. Combine spices, cider, pineapple juice, and sugar in a Dutch oven; bring to a boil. Reduce heat and simmer 15 minutes. Add lemon juice and wine; cook over low heat 10 minutes or just until heated. Remove spice bag. Pour into cups and garnish each with a cinnamon stick. Yield: 11 cups.

HOLIDAY EGGNOG

6 eggs, separated
½ cup sugar
2 cups milk
2 cups whipping cream
½ to 1 cup brandy or bourbon
2 tablespoons dark rum
¼ cup sugar
    Ground nutmeg

Beat egg yolks until thick and lemon colored; gradually add ½ cup sugar and beat until dissolved. Beat in milk, cream, brandy, and rum; cover and refrigerate overnight.

Just before serving, beat egg whites (at room temperature) until soft peaks form. Gradually add ¼ cup sugar, beating until stiff but not dry; gently fold into egg yolk mixture.

Pour into punch bowl and sprinkle with ground nutmeg. Yield: 10 cups.

PLANTATION COFFEE PUNCH

1 quart chocolate milk
½ gallon chocolate, coffee, or vanilla ice
    cream, cubed and softened
2 quarts strong coffee, chilled
    Whipped cream
    Ground nutmeg

Combine first 3 ingredients in a punch bowl; stir until ice cream melts. Garnish with dollops of whipped cream and sprinkle with nutmeg. Yield: 5 quarts.

Sip on our holiday cheer: (clockwise from top) Planter's Punch, Plantation Coffee Punch, Holiday Eggnog, Hot Spiced Cider, Hot Mulled Wine.

Combine lemonade concentrate, orange juice, rum, sugar, and cherry juice in container of electric blender; process at low speed until blended. Pour over coarsely crushed ice in a glass; let stand 10 minutes. Float lemon-lime carbonated beverage on top. Garnish the rim of each glass with an orange slice and a cherry. Yield: 5½ cups.

RUM-CRANBERRY PUNCH

    2 cups light rum
    ½ cup sugar
    1 (12-ounce) can frozen orange juice
         concentrate, thawed and undiluted
    1 (32-ounce) bottle cranberry juice,
         chilled
    1 (33.8-ounce) bottle ginger ale, chilled
         Orange slices
         Strawberries

Combine rum, sugar, orange juice, and cranberry juice. Just before serving, add ginger ale and ice cubes. Garnish with orange slices and strawberries. Yield: about 2½ quarts.

Note: Substitute pineapple juice for rum, if desired.

PLANTER'S PUNCH

    1 (6-ounce) can frozen pink lemonade
         concentrate, undiluted
    1 cup orange juice
    1 cup rum
    1 cup sugar
    1½ teaspoons maraschino cherry juice
    1 (12-ounce) can lemon-lime carbonated
         beverage
         Orange slices
         Maraschino cherries with stems

ORANGE BLOSSOM PUNCH

    1½ quarts orange juice
    1 cup lemon juice
    ⅓ cup maraschino cherry juice
    ½ cup sugar
    1 (33.8-ounce) bottle ginger ale, chilled
         Fresh strawberries (optional)

Combine juices and sugar, mixing well. When ready to serve, add ginger ale; serve over ice. Garnish with fresh strawberries, if desired. Yield: about 3 quarts.

Note: For variation, 2 quarts of lemon or orange sherbet may be added to punch.

81

Breads

FRESH APPLE BREAD

  1 cup sugar
  ½ cup shortening
  2 eggs
  2 cups all-purpose flour
  1 teaspoon soda
  ½ teaspoon salt
1½ tablespoons buttermilk
  ½ teaspoon vanilla extract
  1 cup chopped pecans
  1 tablespoon all-purpose flour
  1 cup peeled and grated apple
1½ tablespoons sugar
  ½ teaspoon ground cinnamon

Combine 1 cup sugar and shortening; cream until light and fluffy. Add eggs, one at a time, beating well after each addition.

Combine 2 cups flour, soda, and salt; combine buttermilk and vanilla. Add dry ingredients to creamed mixture alternately with buttermilk mixture, beating well after each addition.

Combine pecans and 1 tablespoon flour; stir well. Stir pecans and apple into batter. Pour batter into a greased and floured 9- × 5- × 3-inch loafpan. Combine 1½ tablespoons sugar and cinnamon; sprinkle evenly over batter. Bake at 350° for 1 hour. Yield: 1 loaf.

BEST-EVER BANANA BREAD

3½ cups all-purpose flour
2½ teaspoons baking powder
  1 teaspoon soda
1½ teaspoons salt
1⅓ cups sugar
 ⅔ cup shortening
  4 eggs
  2 cups mashed bananas

Combine flour, baking powder, soda, and salt; mix well and set aside.

Combine sugar and shortening; cream until light and fluffy. Add eggs; beat well. Stir in dry ingredients alternately with bananas (do not beat).

Spoon batter into 2 greased and floured 9- × 5- × 3-inch loafpans. Bake at 350° for 45 minutes or until done. Yield: 2 loaves.

CARROT NUT LOAF

1½ cups all-purpose flour
  1 teaspoon soda
  ½ teaspoon salt
  1 teaspoon ground cinnamon
 ¾ cup vegetable oil
  2 eggs
  1 cup sugar
  1 cup grated carrots
  1 cup chopped pecans

Combine first 4 ingredients in a small mixing bowl. Set aside.

Combine oil, eggs, and sugar in a large mixing bowl; beat at medium speed of electric mixer for 1 minute. Add dry ingredients; mix at low speed just until blended. Fold in carrots and pecans. (Batter will be stiff.)

Spoon batter into a greased and floured 8½- × 4½- × 3-inch loafpan; bake at 350° for 1 hour 25 minutes or until bread tests done. Cool 10 minutes in pan; remove to wire rack, and cool completely. Yield: 1 loaf.

A variety of fresh fruits adds flavor to (from left) Best-Ever Banana Bread, Fresh Apple Bread, and Cranberry Bread.

CRANBERRY BREAD

1½ cups fresh cranberries
2 cups all-purpose flour
1 cup sugar
1½ teaspoons baking powder
½ teaspoon soda
1 teaspoon salt
¼ cup butter or margarine
1 egg, beaten
1 teaspoon grated orange rind
¾ cup orange juice
1½ cups golden raisins

Carefully sort and wash cranberries; drain. Grind cranberries coarsely in a food grinder or blender; set aside.

Combine flour, sugar, baking powder, soda, and salt in a large mixing bowl; cut in butter with a pastry blender until mixture resembles coarse crumbs. Add egg, orange rind, and juice; stir until mixture is moistened. Stir in raisins and cranberries; spoon into a greased and floured 9- × 5- × 3-inch loafpan. Bake at 350° for 55 to 60 minutes or until done. Yield: 1 loaf.

CHERRY-NUT SWIRL

- ¼ cup water
- ¼ cup milk
- ½ cup butter
- 1 package dry yeast
- ½ cup sugar
- 3 to 3¼ cups all-purpose flour, divided
- 1 egg
  - Cherry-Nut Filling
  - Glaze (recipe follows)
  - Red and green candied cherries

Combine water, milk, and butter in a small saucepan; cook over low heat until warm (105° to 115°). Dissolve yeast in warm mixture. Combine yeast mixture, sugar, 1 cup flour, and egg in a large mixing bowl; beat at low speed of electric mixer 2 minutes. Gradually stir in enough remaining flour to make a soft dough. Cover and let rise in a warm place (85°), free from drafts, until doubled in bulk.

Punch down dough and turn out onto a floured surface; knead lightly 6 to 8 times to form a smooth ball. Cover and let rest 15 minutes.

Roll out dough into a 12- × 10-inch rectangle. Spread Cherry-Nut Filling evenly over rectangle, leaving a 1-inch margin. Roll up dough lengthwise; pinch seam and ends to seal. Place roll, seam side down, on a greased baking sheet.

Cover and let rise in a warm place, free from drafts, until doubled in bulk. Bake at 350° for 40 to 50 minutes or until loaf sounds hollow when tapped.

Drizzle with glaze and decorate with candied cherries. Yield: 1 loaf.

Cherry-Nut Filling:

- ¾ cup whole almonds, ground
- ¼ cup finely chopped candied cherries
- ¼ cup plus 2 tablespoons honey
- 2 tablespoons milk
- ½ teaspoon ground cinnamon
- ¼ teaspoon almond extract
- ¼ teaspoon vanilla extract

Combine all ingredients; stir well. Yield: 1 cup.

Glaze:

- 1 cup sifted powdered sugar
- 1½ to 2 tablespoons milk

Combine sugar and milk; stir until smooth. Yield: about ½ cup.

FRENCH LEMON SPIRALS

- 1 package dry yeast
- 2¼ to 2½ cups all-purpose flour, divided
- ½ cup milk
- ¼ cup plus 2 tablespoons butter or margarine
- ¼ cup sugar
- ¼ teaspoon salt
- 2 eggs
- 2 teaspoons grated lemon rind
- ¼ cup butter or margarine, softened
- ½ cup sugar
- 2 teaspoons grated lemon rind

Combine yeast and 1 cup flour in a large mixing bowl. Combine milk, ¼ cup plus 2 tablespoons butter, ¼ cup sugar, and salt in a saucepan; cook over low heat until butter melts. Cool to lukewarm (105° to 115°). Stir into flour mixture, blending well. Add eggs, and 2 teaspoons lemon rind; beat at low speed of electric mixer until blended. Beat at high speed 3 minutes. Stir in enough of remaining flour to make a stiff dough. Cover and chill 2 to 3 hours.

Divide dough in half; turn out onto a lightly floured surface. Roll each half into a 12- × 7-inch rectangle. Spread each with 2 tablespoons butter, and sprinkle each with ¼ cup sugar and 1 teaspoon lemon rind. Roll up dough jellyroll fashion, starting at the long side; pinch seam to seal. Cut each roll into 12 slices and place on greased baking sheets.

Cover and let rise in a warm place (85°), free from drafts, until doubled in bulk, about 1 hour. Bake at 375° for 12 minutes or until lightly browned. Yield: 2 dozen.

Nothing tops a cup of coffee and breads fresh from the oven: (clockwise from top) Swedish Tea Ring, Cherry-Nut Swirl, French Lemon Spirals.

SWEDISH TEA RING

  1 package dry yeast
  ¼ cup warm water (105° to 115°)
  1 cup whipping cream
  ¼ cup evaporated milk
  3 egg yolks, slightly beaten
  ½ cup butter, melted
  3 to 3½ cups all-purpose flour
  ¼ cup sugar
  1 teaspoon salt
  2 tablespoons butter, softened
    Filling (recipe follows)
  1 egg white, slightly beaten
  1 tablespoon sugar
    Glaze (recipe follows)
    Sliced almonds
    Red candied cherries

Dissolve yeast in warm water in a medium bowl; stir in cream, milk, egg yolks, and melted butter.

Combine flour, ¼ cup sugar, and salt in a large bowl; add yeast mixture and blend well. Place dough in a greased bowl, turning to grease top. Cover and let rise in a warm place (85°), free from drafts, for 1 hour or until doubled in bulk.

Turn dough out onto a lightly floured surface and knead lightly until smooth. Roll dough to a 24- × 20-inch rectangle. Brush dough with softened butter and spread with filling, leaving a 1-inch margin. Roll up dough jellyroll fashion, starting at long side; press seam to seal. Place on a large greased baking sheet, seam side down. Shape into a ring, and pinch ends together to seal. With kitchen shears or a sharp knife, make a cut every inch around ring (cut should go two-thirds of way through roll). Gently pull slices out and twist, overlapping slices slightly. Brush with egg white and sprinkle with 1 tablespoon sugar. Cover and let rise in a warm place (85°), for 1 hour or until doubled in bulk. Bake at 350° for 20 to 25 minutes. Cool on wire rack; drizzle glaze on top and decorate with almonds and cherries. Yield: 1 large coffee ring.

Filling:

  1 cup walnut halves or pieces
  ½ cup sugar
  1 tablespoon ground cinnamon

Combine all ingredients in container of an electric blender; blend until finely ground. Yield: about 1 cup.

Glaze:

  1 cup sifted powdered sugar
  1½ tablespoons milk

Combine sugar and milk, stirring until smooth. Yield: about ½ cup.

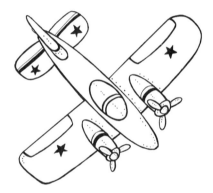

HONEY OATMEAL BUNS

  ¼ cup sugar
  2 packages dry yeast
  2 teaspoons salt
  1 cup regular oats, uncooked
  4½ to 5 cups all-purpose flour, divided
  ½ cup water
  1 cup milk
  ¼ cup butter or margarine
  2 eggs
    Honey Topping
  ⅔ cup chopped pecans
  ¼ cup butter or margarine, melted
  ½ cup firmly packed brown sugar
  2 teaspoons ground cinnamon

Combine sugar, yeast, salt, oats, and 1½ cups flour in large bowl. Set aside.

Heat water, milk, and ¼ cup butter in a small saucepan to 120° to 130°. Add to dry ingredients; beat 2 minutes at medium speed of mixer, scraping bowl occasionally. Add 1 cup flour and eggs; beat 2 minutes at high speed. Stir in enough remaining flour to make a soft dough.

Turn dough out onto a lightly floured surface and knead until smooth and elastic, about 8 to 10 minutes. Place in a greased bowl, turning to grease top. Cover; let rise in a warm place (85°), free from drafts, for 1 hour or until doubled in bulk. Punch dough down. Let rest 10 minutes.

Prepare Honey Topping; pour into two lightly greased 9-inch-square nonstick pans. Tilt pans to cover evenly. Sprinkle half of pecans in each pan. Set aside.

Divide dough in half. Roll one half into a 12- × 9-inch rectangle on a lightly floured board. Brush with half of melted butter. Combine brown sugar and cinnamon; stir. Sprinkle half of cinnamon mixture on each rectangle, leaving a ½-inch margin on all sides. Roll up each rectangle, starting at long end, jellyroll fashion. Pinch edge and ends to seal. Cut each roll into twelve 1-inch slices. Arrange cut side down in prepared pans. Cover and let rise until doubled in bulk.

Bake at 375° for 25 minutes. Cool 5 minutes on a rack; invert onto plate. Yield: 2 dozen.

Honey Topping:

½ cup honey
½ cup firmly packed brown sugar
¼ cup butter or margarine
¼ teaspoon salt

Combine ingredients in a small saucepan; bring to a boil, stirring constantly. Simmer for 1½ to 2 minutes. Yield: about 1 cup.

Cakes & Fruitcakes

FRESH APPLE SPICE CAKE

1 cup vegetable oil
2 cups sugar
3 eggs
3 cups all-purpose flour
1 teaspoon soda
¼ teaspoon salt
1 teaspoon ground cinnamon
1 teaspoon ground nutmeg
1 teaspoon vanilla extract
1 cup chopped pecans
3 cups peeled, finely chopped apples
Glaze (recipe follows)

Combine oil and sugar; beat well. Add eggs, one at a time, beating well after each addition. Combine flour, soda, salt, cinnamon, and nutmeg; stir. Add dry ingredients to sugar mixture, beating well. Add vanilla; mix well. Stir in pecans and apples. Pour batter into a greased and floured 10-inch tube pan. Bake at 350° for 1 hour and 15 minutes or until cake tests done.

Using a wooden pick, punch holes in cake while hot; spoon glaze over cake. Cool; remove from pan. Yield: one 10-inch cake.

Glaze:

½ cup sugar
¼ cup buttermilk
¼ teaspoon soda
2 tablespoons butter or margarine
1½ teaspoons vanilla extract

Combine all ingredients in a medium saucepan. Bring to a boil; boil 4 minutes, stirring occasionally. Yield: about ¾ cup.

COCONUT POUND CAKE

    1 cup butter or margarine
    ½ cup shortening
    3 cups sugar
    6 eggs
    1 teaspoon coconut flavoring
    ½ teaspoon almond extract
    3 cups all-purpose flour
    1 cup milk
    1 (3½-ounce) can flaked coconut

Cream butter, shortening, and sugar until light and fluffy. Add eggs, one at a time, beating well after each addition. Add flavorings and mix well. Alternately add flour and milk, beating after each addition. Stir in coconut. Spoon the batter into a greased 10-inch tube pan or Bundt pan. Bake at 350° for 1 hour and 15 minutes. Yield: 1 (10-inch) cake.

OLD-FASHIONED SPICE CAKE

    1 (15-ounce) package raisins
    3 cups hot water
    2 cups sugar
    1 cup butter or margarine
    ½ teaspoon ground cinnamon
    ¼ teaspoon ground cloves
    5 cups all-purpose flour
    1 tablespoon soda

Combine first 6 ingredients in a large Dutch oven; bring to a boil, and boil 5 minutes. Cool. Combine flour and soda; gradually stir into cooled mixture, mixing well. Pour into greased and floured 10-inch tube pan. Bake at 325° for 70 to 75 minutes. Yield: one 10-inch cake.

CHRISTMAS PLUM PUDDING

    1 cup all-purpose flour
    1 teaspoon soda
    1 teaspoon salt
    1 teaspoon ground cinnamon
    ½ teaspoon ground nutmeg
    ½ teaspoon ground allspice
    1½ cups chopped raisins
    1½ cups currants
    1 cup diced citron
    ¾ cup mixed diced candied lemon and
          orange peel
    ½ cup chopped almonds
    1½ cups soft breadcrumbs
    1 cup firmly packed brown sugar
    3 eggs, beaten
    ⅓ cup currant jelly
    ¼ cup sherry or brandy
    2 cups ground suet
       Hard sauce (recipe follows)

Combine flour, soda, salt, and spices. Add fruit, almonds, and breadcrumbs; mix well.

Combine brown sugar, eggs, jelly, and sherry; add to fruit mixture along with suet, mixing well. Pack mixture into a well-buttered and sugared 1½-quart mold; cover tightly with aluminum foil.

Place mold on shallow rack in a large, deep kettle with enough boiling water to come halfway up the mold. Cover kettle; steam pudding about 5½ hours in continuously boiling water (replace water as needed). (If desired, wrap securely, and store in refrigerator several weeks to allow to ripen.) Unmold and serve with hard sauce. Yield: 12 servings.

Hard Sauce:

    ½ cup butter or margarine, softened
    1 cup powdered sugar
    ¼ cup brandy

Combine butter and powdered sugar; beat until smooth. Add brandy and beat until fluffy. Chill. Yield: 1 cup.

Christmas Plum Pudding is a blend of fruits, nuts, and spices served with a brandy-flavored hard sauce; some people make it months ahead to let it mellow.

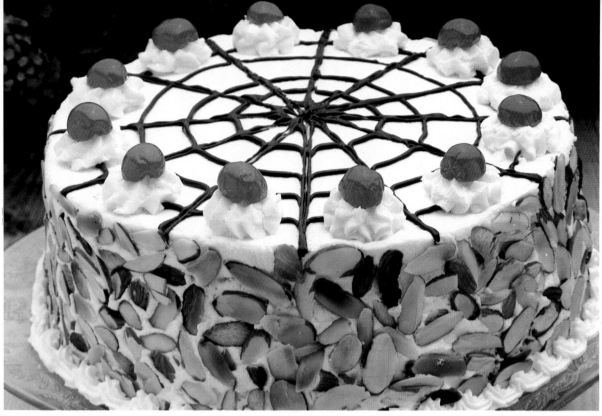

Almond Butter Cake is simple to decorate and to serve; just slice it along the chocolate lines.

ALMOND BUTTER CAKE

- 1 **cup butter, softened**
- 2 **cups sugar**
- 4 **eggs**
- 3 **cups all-purpose flour**
- 2 **teaspoons baking powder**
- 1 **teaspoon salt**
- 1 **cup milk**
- 1 **teaspoon vanilla extract**
- ½ **teaspoon almond extract**
- ½ **teaspoon butter flavoring**
  Buttercream Frosting
- 2 **(1-ounce) squares semisweet chocolate**
- 1½ **cups sliced almonds, toasted**
- 6 **maraschino cherries, halved**

Cream butter; gradually add sugar, beating until light and fluffy and sugar is dissolved. Add eggs, one at a time, beating well after each addition.

Combine flour, baking powder, and salt; add to creamed mixture alternately with milk, beginning and ending with flour mixture. Beat on low speed of electric mixer just until blended. Stir in flavorings.

Pour batter into 2 greased and floured 9-inch round cakepans. Bake at 350° for 30 to 35 minutes or until cake tests done. Cool in pans 10 minutes; remove from pans and complete cooling on wire racks.

Spread Buttercream Frosting between layers and on top and sides of cake, reserving about 1 cup frosting for decorating. Smooth sides and top of cake using a wet metal spatula.

Melt chocolate in the top of a double boiler over hot water. Prepare a decorating bag with metal decorating tip No. 4; spoon chocolate into bag. Pipe chocolate in 5 graduated circles around top of cake. Pull the point of a toothpick across the chocolate circles from the center to the outer edge, making 12 lines spaced evenly across top of cake.

Press almonds into icing around sides of cake. Prepare a decorating bag with metal decorating tip No. 18; spoon reserved frosting into bag. Pipe a zigzag border around base of cake. Pipe drop flowers onto top of cake at wide end of each triangle created by chocolate. Top each flower with a cherry half. Yield: one 9-inch cake.

Buttercream Frosting:

    1 cup shortening
    ½ teaspoon salt
    1 teaspoon almond extract or butter
         flavoring
    ½ cup water
    1 (16-ounce) package powdered sugar,
         sifted
  1¾ cups sifted powdered sugar

Combine shortening, salt, and extract in a large mixing bowl; beat at medium speed of electric mixer until blended. Alternately add small amounts of water and powdered sugar, beating constantly at low speed until blended. Beat 8 minutes at medium speed of electric mixer. Yield: about 3½ cups.

FAVORITE CHOCOLATE CAKE

    ½ cup shortening
    2 cups sugar
    2 eggs
    4 (1-ounce) squares unsweetened
         chocolate, melted
    2 cups sifted cake flour
    ½ teaspoon baking powder
    1 teaspoon soda
    1 teaspoon salt
    ¾ cup buttermilk
    ¾ cup water
    1 teaspoon vanilla extract
         Chocolate Filling (recipe follows)
         Chocolate Frosting (recipe follows)

Cream shortening; gradually add sugar, beating well. Add eggs, one at a time, beating well after each addition. Add chocolate, mixing well.

Combine flour, baking powder, soda, and salt; gradually add to chocolate mixture alternately with buttermilk, beating well after each addition. Add water, mixing well; stir in vanilla.

Line bottom of two greased 9-inch round cakepans with waxed paper. Pour batter evenly into pans; bake at 350° for 30 minutes or until a wooden pick inserted in center comes out clean. Cool in pans 10 minutes; remove from pans, and place on wire racks to complete cooling.

Spread chocolate filling between layers. Frost top and sides of cake with chocolate frosting. Yield: one 2-layer cake.

Chocolate Filling:

    2 tablespoons cornstarch
    ½ cup sugar
         Dash of salt
    ½ cup water
    1 tablespoon butter or margarine
    2 (1-ounce) squares semisweet
         chocolate

Combine cornstarch, sugar, salt, and water in small saucepan; cook over medium heat, stirring constantly, until thickened. Remove from heat. Add butter and chocolate; stir until melted. Let cool. Yield: filling for one 2-layer cake.

Chocolate Frosting:

    2 cups sugar
    1 cup evaporated milk
    ½ cup butter or margarine
    1 (6-ounce) package semisweet
         chocolate morsels
    1 cup marshmallow creme
    2 tablespoons milk
    1 tablespoon light corn syrup

Combine sugar, milk, and butter in a medium saucepan; cook over medium heat, stirring constantly, until mixture reaches soft ball stage (234°). Remove from heat; add remaining ingredients, stirring until smooth and chocolate is melted. Let cool slightly; beat until of spreading consistency. Yield: frosting for one 2-layer cake.

GERMAN CHOCOLATE CAKE

    1 (4-ounce) package sweet baking
      chocolate
  ½ cup water
    1 teaspoon vanilla extract
    1 cup shortening
    2 cups sugar
    4 eggs, separated
2½ cups sifted cake flour
    1 teaspoon soda
      Pinch of salt
    1 cup buttermilk
      Coconut-Pecan Frosting
      Pecan halves (optional)

Combine chocolate and water; bring to a boil, and stir until chocolate melts. Cool; stir in vanilla, and set aside.

Cream shortening; gradually add sugar, beating until light and fluffy. Add egg yolks, one at a time, beating well after each addition. Add chocolate mixture; beat until blended.

Combine flour, soda, and salt; add to creamed mixture alternately with buttermilk, beginning and ending with the flour mixture. Beat the egg whites (at room temperature) until stiff peaks form; fold in.

Pour batter into 3 greased and floured 9-inch round cakepans. Bake at 350° for 30 to 35 minutes or until a wooden pick inserted in center comes out clean. Cool 10 minutes; remove from pans, and cool completely.

Spread Coconut-Pecan Frosting between layers and on top and sides of cake. Garnish with pecan halves, if desired. Yield: one 3-layer cake.

Coconut-Pecan Frosting

1⅓ cups evaporated milk
1½ cups sugar
    4 egg yolks
  ¾ cup butter or margarine
    1 teaspoon vanilla extract
1½ cups flaked coconut
  ¾ cup chopped pecans

Combine milk, sugar, egg yolks, and butter in a heavy saucepan; bring to a boil, and cook over medium heat for 12 minutes, stirring constantly. Add vanilla, coconut, and pecans; stir until frosting is cool and of spreading consistency. Yield: enough for one 3-layer cake.

SALLY WHITE CAKE

    1 cup butter, softened
1½ cups sugar
    6 egg yolks
    2 tablespoons bourbon
    2 tablespoons sherry
    1 pound candied citron
  ½ pound blanched almonds
    1 (7-ounce) can flaked coconut
    2 cups all-purpose flour
  ½ teaspoon ground nutmeg
    1 teaspoon ground mace
    6 egg whites, stiffly beaten
      Wine jelly (recipe follows)
      Whipped cream

Cream butter and sugar until light and fluffy. Add egg yolks, bourbon, and sherry; beat until light yellow.

Combine citron, almonds, and coconut in container of an electric blender; blend until finely chopped, and stir into creamed mixture. Combine flour, nutmeg, and mace; add to creamed mixture, beating well. Fold in egg whites.

Spoon batter into a lightly greased and floured 10-inch Bundt pan. Bake at 250° for 3 hours. Turn out on rack to cool. Serve slices with wine jelly; top with whipped cream. Yield: one 10-inch cake.

Serve Sally White Cake with wine jelly for a traditional and elegant holiday dessert.

Wine Jelly:

2⅔ cups boiling water
  Grated rind and juice of 2 lemons
  2 small sticks cinnamon
  2 envelopes unflavored gelatin
  ¼ cup cold water
  1 cup sugar
  1 cup sherry

Combine boiling water, lemon rind and juice, and cinnamon; simmer for 5 minutes.

Soften gelatin in cold water for 5 minutes; add softened gelatin and sugar to hot mixture, mixing well. Strain through cheesecloth. Cool. Stir in sherry. Refrigerate. Yield: about 4 cups.

Confections

BUTTER MINTS

  1 **(3-ounce) package cream cheese, softened**
  2 **teaspoons butter flavoring**
 ⅛ **teaspoon oil of peppermint**
  1 **(16-ounce) package powdered sugar**
     Yellow paste food coloring

Combine first 4 ingredients; beat at low speed of electric mixer until blended. Add a small amount of food coloring and mix until blended.

Press mixture into mint molds or roll into small balls and flatten slightly. Yield: about 7 dozen.

CANDY-STUFFED DATES

  2 **tablespoons plus 2 teaspoons margarine**
 ¼ **cup light corn syrup**
1¾ **cups sifted powdered sugar, divided**
 ½ **teaspoon vanilla extract**
     Paste food coloring
  2 **(8-ounce) packages pitted dates**

Combine margarine, corn syrup, and 1 cup powdered sugar in a saucepan; bring to a boil over medium heat, stirring constantly. Remove from heat. Add remaining sugar and vanilla, stirring just until mixture holds its shape. Pour into a greased jellyroll pan to cool. Knead cooled candy until smooth. Knead in food coloring as desired.

Make a lengthwise slit in dates. Stuff dates with candy mixture. Yield: about 6½ dozen.

Christmas isn't Christmas without candy: (clockwise from top) Peanut Butter Fudge, Fruit Roll, Butter Mints, Candy-Stuffed Dates, Deluxe Peanut Brittle.

PEANUT BUTTER FUDGE

1 (12-ounce) jar creamy peanut butter
1 (7½-ounce) jar marshmallow creme
1 teaspoon vanilla extract
1 cup chopped salted peanuts
2 cups sugar
2 cups firmly packed light brown sugar
¾ cup milk
½ teaspoon salt
¼ cup salted peanut halves

Combine peanut butter, marshmallow creme, vanilla, and chopped peanuts in a large bowl; set aside.

Combine sugar, milk, and salt; stir well. Cook over medium heat until mixture comes to a boil; boil 4 minutes, stirring occasionally. Remove from heat and pour over peanut butter mixture; stir quickly until well blended. Pour into a buttered 13- × 9- × 2-inch pan and sprinkle with peanut halves. Allow candy to cool for at least 2 hours. Cut fudge into squares. Yield: 3½ dozen.

FRUIT ROLL

1 (12-ounce) package vanilla wafers, crushed
1 cup chopped candied pineapple
1 cup chopped candied cherries
2 cups chopped pecans or walnuts
1 (14-ounce) can sweetened condensed milk
Sifted powdered sugar

Combine first 5 ingredients, mixing well. Divide into 3 equal portions; roll each into an 11-inch log. Roll each log in powdered sugar and wrap in plastic. Refrigerate several hours or until firm; cut into ½-inch slices, reshaping slices if necessary. Yield: about 5 dozen.

DELUXE PEANUT BRITTLE

3 cups sugar
1 cup light corn syrup
½ cup water
1 pound raw peanuts
3 tablespoons butter or margarine
1½ teaspoons soda
1 teaspoon salt
1½ teaspoons vanilla extract

Combine sugar, corn syrup, and water in a Dutch oven; cook over low heat to soft crack stage (270°). Stir in peanuts; cook to hard crack stage (300°). Remove from heat. Stir in butter, soda, salt, and vanilla.

Pour into 2 warm buttered 15- × 10- × 1-inch jellyroll pans, and spread to edges of pans. Cool and break into pieces. Yield: 3 pounds.

NUT CLUSTERS

1 (7-ounce) jar marshmallow creme
1½ pounds milk chocolate kisses
5 cups sugar
1 (13-ounce) can evaporated milk
½ cup butter or margarine
6 cups pecan or walnut halves

Place marshmallow creme and kisses in a large bowl; set aside. Combine sugar, milk, and butter in a saucepan. Bring mixture to a boil; then cook for 8 minutes. Pour over marshmallow creme and kisses, stirring until well blended. Stir in pecans. Drop by teaspoonfuls onto waxed paper. Yield: about 12 dozen.

GLAZED PECANS

½ cup half-and-half
¼ cup water
1 cup sugar
1 teaspoon vanilla extract
4 cups pecan halves

Combine all ingredients except pecans in a medium saucepan; stir well. Place over medium heat, stirring constantly, until sugar dissolves; continue cooking until mixture registers about 220° on candy thermometer. Remove from heat; add pecans, stirring until well coated.

Spread pecans on waxed paper and separate with a fork. Cool. Yield: 4 cups.

CHOCOLATE BALLS

1 tablespoon cocoa
½ cup powdered sugar
¼ cup bourbon
1 tablespoon light corn syrup
½ cup finely ground pecans or walnuts
1¼ cups finely crushed vanilla wafers
2 egg whites, slightly beaten
12 ounces chocolate sprinkles

Sift cocoa and sugar together; set aside. Combine bourbon and corn syrup in a bowl; stir in cocoa mixture, pecans, and vanilla wafers.

Roll mixture into 1-inch balls. Dip each ball into egg white, and roll in chocolate sprinkles. Store in a covered container. These freeze well. Yield: about 20.

Cookies

HOLLY SQUARES

1 cup all-purpose flour
1 teaspoon baking powder
½ teaspoon salt
½ cup butter or margarine, melted
1 egg
½ cup evaporated milk
½ cup sugar
1 cup firmly packed brown sugar
1 cup regular oats, uncooked
1 cup chopped pecans or walnuts
1 cup chopped dates
¼ cup chopped mixed candied fruit
   Glaze (recipe follows)
   Red and green candied cherries

Combine first 3 ingredients in a large bowl. Add next 5 ingredients; beat until blended. Stir in oats, pecans, dates, and candied fruit. Spread mixture in a greased 13- × 9- × 2-inch pan. Bake at 350° for 45 to 50 minutes. Cool. Drizzle with glaze; cut into squares and decorate with cherries. Yield: 2 dozen.

Glaze:

1 cup sifted powdered sugar
¼ teaspoon salt
2 tablespoons milk
½ teaspoon vanilla extract

Combine all ingredients and stir until smooth. Yield: about ½ cup.

Package homemade cookies as gifts for family or friends: (top, left to right) Neopolitan Cookies, Chocolate Kiss Cookies, Tiger Cookies, Date-Nut Cookies, Holly Squares.

DATE-NUT COOKIES

    1 cup chopped pecans or walnuts
    1 cup chopped dates
    1 cup chopped candied cherries
    ¼ cup all-purpose flour
    ¼ cup milk
    1 teaspoon cider vinegar
    ½ cup butter, softened
    1 cup firmly packed brown sugar
    1 egg
 1½ cups all-purpose flour
    ¼ teaspoon salt
    ½ teaspoon soda

Combine first 4 ingredients, tossing well; set aside. Combine milk and vinegar and let stand 10 minutes. Cream butter and brown sugar until light and fluffy; add egg, mixing well. Combine 1½ cups flour, salt, and soda; add to creamed mixture alternately with milk mixture. Stir in fruit mixture.

Drop dough by heaping teaspoonfuls onto ungreased cookie sheets. Bake at 375° for 10 minutes or until golden brown. Remove from pans immediately and cool on wire racks. Yield: about 4 dozen.

TIGER COOKIES

    ¾ cup margarine, softened
    1 cup sugar
    2 eggs
    1 teaspoon vanilla extract
    2 cups all-purpose flour
    1 teaspoon soda
    ½ teaspoon salt
    3 cups sugar-frosted flake cereal,
        crushed
    1 (6-ounce) package semisweet
        chocolate morsels

Cream margarine and sugar in a large mixing bowl until light and fluffy; beat in eggs and vanilla. Combine flour, soda, and salt; add to creamed mixture, mixing well. Stir in crushed cereal. Melt chocolate in the top of a double boiler. Swirl melted chocolate lightly through dough, leaving streaks of chocolate.

Drop dough by heaping teaspoonfuls onto ungreased cookie sheets. Bake at 375° for 10 to 12 minutes. Cool on wire racks. Yield: 5 dozen.

NEOPOLITAN COOKIES

    1 cup butter or margarine, softened
 1½ cups sugar
    1 egg
    1 teaspoon vanilla extract
 2½ cups all-purpose flour
 1½ teaspoons baking powder
    ½ teaspoon salt
    ½ teaspoon almond extract
        Red food coloring
    ½ cup chopped pecans or walnuts
    1 (1-ounce) square unsweetened
        chocolate, melted

Cream butter; gradually add sugar, beating until light and fluffy. Add egg and vanilla; beat well. Combine flour, baking powder, and salt; add to creamed mixture, beating just until blended.

Line bottom and sides of a 9- × 5- × 3-inch loafpan with waxed paper. Spoon ⅓ of dough into a small bowl; add almond extract and 5 drops red food coloring, stirring until blended; spread evenly into prepared pan. Spoon half of remaining dough into a small bowl; stir in pecans. Spread evenly over dough in pan. Melt chocolate in the top of a double boiler; stir into remaining dough and spread evenly over dough in pan. Cover and refrigerate overnight.

Remove dough from pan and peel off waxed paper. Cut dough lengthwise in half; slice each half crosswise into ⅛-inch slices. Place slices on ungreased cookie sheets, 1 inch apart. Bake at 350° for 10 to 12 minutes. Cool on wire racks. Yield: 5 dozen.

CHOCOLATE KISS COOKIES

1¼ cups margarine, softened
1 cup sugar
2 eggs
½ teaspoon vanilla extract
3¼ cups all-purpose flour
1 (14-ounce) package chocolate kisses

Cream margarine; gradually add sugar, beating until light and fluffy. Add eggs and vanilla; blend well. Stir in flour.

Spoon dough into a cookie press with a star or daisy-shaped disc. Press cookies onto un-greased cookie sheets. Bake at 375° for 10 minutes. Immediately press one chocolate kiss in center of each cookie, point side up. Remove from pan and cool on wire racks. Yield: 6 dozen.

GINGER CRINKLES

⅔ cup vegetable oil
1 cup sugar
1 egg
¼ cup molasses
2 cups all-purpose flour
½ teaspoon salt
2 teaspoons soda
1 teaspoon ground cinnamon
1 teaspoon ground ginger
¼ cup sugar

Combine oil and 1 cup sugar in a large mixing bowl; add egg and beat well. Stir in molasses. Combine flour, salt, soda, cinnamon, and ginger; add to molasses mixture, stirring to mix. Roll dough into 1-inch balls; roll each in remaining ¼ cup sugar. Place 2 inches apart on greased cookie sheets. Bake at 350° for 10 to 12 minutes or until lightly browned. Remove to wire rack to cool. Yield: about 4 dozen.

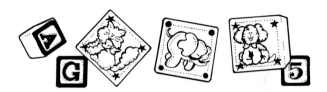

PEANUT BUTTER SQUARES

1 cup all-purpose flour
½ cup sugar
½ cup firmly packed brown sugar
½ teaspoon soda
¼ teaspoon salt
½ cup butter or margarine, softened
⅓ cup crunchy or smooth peanut butter
1 egg
1 cup quick-cooking oats, uncooked
1 (12-ounce) package semisweet
  chocolate morsels
½ cup sifted powdered sugar
¼ cup smooth peanut butter
3 to 5 tablespoons milk

Combine first 9 ingredients in a large mixing bowl; mix well.

Press dough into a lightly greased 13- × 9- × 2-inch pan. Bake at 350° for 20 minutes. Remove from oven and sprinkle with chocolate morsels. Let stand 5 minutes or until chocolate has melted; spread evenly.

Combine powdered sugar, ¼ cup smooth peanut butter, and enough milk to make a thin consistency; beat well. Drizzle over cookies. Cut into squares. Yield: about 2 dozen.

Pies

BLACK BOTTOM ICE CREAM PIE

1 cup chocolate ice cream, softened
Gingersnap Crumb Crust
Creamy Chocolate Sauce
1 quart vanilla ice cream, softened

Spread chocolate ice cream in bottom of crust; freeze until firm. Spread half of cooled Creamy Chocolate Sauce over ice cream in crust; freeze until set. Spoon vanilla ice cream over chocolate sauce; freeze until firm. Drizzle remaining chocolate sauce evenly over pie; freeze until ready to serve. Yield: one 9-inch pie.

Gingersnap Crumb Crust:

1½ cups gingersnap crumbs
¼ cup powdered sugar
⅓ cup butter or margarine, melted

Combine all ingredients, mixing well. Press firmly onto bottom and sides of a 9-inch piepan. Chill well. Yield: one 9-inch crust.

Creamy Chocolate Sauce:

1 (6-ounce) package semisweet
    chocolate morsels
½ cup whipping cream
½ teaspoon vanilla extract

Combine chocolate morsels and cream in a small, heavy saucepan; place over low heat until chocolate melts, stirring constantly. Remove from heat, and stir in vanilla. Cool completely. Yield: about 1 cup.

HEAVENLY PIE

4 eggs, separated
¼ teaspoon cream of tartar
1 cup sugar
½ cup sugar
3 tablespoons fresh lemon juice
1 tablespoon grated lemon rind
⅛ teaspoon salt
2 cups whipping cream, whipped

Beat egg whites (at room temperature) until frothy; add cream of tartar, beating slightly. Gradually add 1 cup sugar, beating well after each addition; continue beating until stiff and glossy. Do not underbeat.

Spoon meringue into a well-greased 9-inch piepan. Use a spoon to shape meringue into a pie shell, swirling sides high. Bake at 275° for 50 minutes. Cool.

Beat egg yolks until thick and lemon colored. Gradually add ½ cup sugar, lemon juice, lemon rind, and salt. Cook in top of a double boiler, stirring constantly, until smooth and thickened. Cool.

Fold half of whipped cream into lemon mixture; spoon into meringue shell and spread evenly. Cover and refrigerate at least 12 hours. Top with remaining whipped cream. Yield: one 9-inch pie.

PUMPKIN-ICE CREAM PIE

1 pint vanilla ice cream, softened
1 baked 10-inch pastry shell
1 (16-ounce) can pumpkin
1½ cups sugar
    Dash of salt
½ to 1 teaspoon ground ginger
1 teaspoon ground cinnamon
1 teaspoon vanilla extract
1½ cups whipping cream, divided
    Caramelized Almonds (recipe follows)

Spread ice cream in bottom of pastry shell; freeze until firm. Combine pumpkin, sugar, salt,

Pumpkin-Ice Cream Pie, garnished with whipped cream and caramelized almonds, is a fitting finale for a traditional holiday dinner.

spices, and vanilla; stir well. Beat 1 cup whipping cream until light and fluffy; fold into pumpkin mixture. Spread over ice cream layer; freeze until firm.

Beat remaining whipping cream until light and fluffy, and use to garnish frozen pie just before serving. Sprinkle with Caramelized Almonds. Yield: one 10-inch pie.

Caramelized Almonds:

¼ cup sugar
1 cup slivered almonds

Combine sugar and almonds; cook over low heat until sugar and almonds have browned, stirring constantly. Spread mixture in a thin layer on a buttered cookie sheet; cool. Break into small pieces. Yield: 1 cup.

DEEP-DISH APPLE PIE

    8 cooking apples, peeled and thinly
      sliced
 1¼ cups sugar
    3 tablespoons all-purpose flour
 1½ teaspoons ground cinnamon
  ¼ teaspoon ground nutmeg
  ⅛ teaspoon salt
    3 tablespoons butter or margarine
      Pastry (recipe follows)

Arrange apple slices in a lightly greased 9-inch-square baking dish. Combine sugar, flour, cinnamon, nutmeg, and salt; sprinkle over apples, and dot with butter. Top with pastry, and bake at 400° for 40 minutes or until golden brown. Yield: 6 to 8 servings.

Pastry:

 1¼ cups all-purpose flour
  ¼ teaspoon salt
    2 tablespoons shortening
  ¼ cup cold butter or margarine
    3 to 4 tablespoons cold water

Combine flour and salt; cut in shortening. Cut butter into small pieces, and add to flour mixture; cut in until mixture resembles coarse meal. Stir in only enough water to moisten flour; form dough into a ball. Wrap in plastic wrap, and chill 30 minutes.

Roll dough to ¼-inch thickness on a lightly floured surface, and cut into 1-inch-wide strips. Arrange lattice fashion over filling. Yield: pastry for one 9-inch pie.

PECAN TARTS

  ¾ cup firmly packed light brown sugar
    1 tablespoon butter or margarine,
      melted
    1 egg, slightly beaten
    1 teaspoon vanilla extract
  ⅔ cup chopped pecans
      Cream Cheese Shells

Combine first 5 ingredients, mixing well; spoon 1 teaspoonful filling into each pastry shell.

Bake tarts at 350° for 17 minutes. Yield: 2 dozen.

Cream Cheese Shells:

    1 (3-ounce) package cream cheese,
      softened
  ½ cup butter or margarine, softened
    1 cup all-purpose flour

Combine cream cheese and butter; cream until smooth. Add flour, mixing well. Refrigerate dough 1 hour; then shape into 24 balls.

Put each ball in a greased miniature muffin tin, shaping into a shell. Bake at 350° for 15 minutes before filling. Yield: 2 dozen.

PINEAPPLE MERINGUE PIE

    3 eggs, separated
    1 cup sugar
  ¼ cup plus 1 tablespoon all-purpose
      flour
    2 cups crushed pineapple, undrained
    1 teaspoon lemon juice
  ⅛ teaspoon salt
    1 tablespoon butter or margarine
    1 baked 9-inch pastry shell
    1 tablespoon water
  ¼ teaspoon cream of tartar
  ¾ teaspoon vanilla extract
  ¼ cup plus 2 tablespoons sugar

Beat egg yolks. Combine yolks, 1 cup sugar, flour, pineapple, lemon juice, and salt in top of double boiler; stir well. Cook over boiling water, stirring constantly, until thickened. Remove from heat; stir in butter. Pour mixture into pastry shell.

Combine egg whites, water, cream of tartar, and vanilla extract in a small mixing bowl; beat until foamy. Gradually add remaining sugar; continue beating until stiff peaks form. Spread meringue over pie and seal edges carefully. Bake at 400° about 10 minutes or until lightly browned. Cool. Refrigerate pie until chilled. Yield: one 9-inch pie.

COCONUT CREAM PIE

¾ cup sugar
3 tablespoons cornstarch
¼ teaspoon salt
2 cups milk
3 eggs, separated
2 tablespoons butter or margarine
1 teaspoon vanilla extract
1 (3½-ounce) can flaked coconut
1 baked 9-inch pastry shell
½ teaspoon vanilla extract
¼ teaspoon cream of tartar
¼ cup plus 2 tablespoons sugar

Combine ¾ cup sugar, cornstarch, and salt in a medium saucepan; gradually stir in milk. Cook over medium heat, stirring constantly, until thickened. Beat egg yolks; add a small amount of hot mixture to egg yolks, beating well. Stir egg mixture into hot mixture. Cook and stir over medium heat 2 minutes. Remove from heat; stir in butter, 1 teaspoon vanilla, and 1 cup coconut. Spoon mixture into pastry shell.

Beat egg whites, ½ teaspoon vanilla, and cream of tartar until foamy. Gradually add remaining sugar; continue beating until stiff peaks form. Spread meringue over pie, being careful to seal edges. Sprinkle remaining coconut over top. Bake at 350° about 10 minutes or until lightly browned. Cool. Refrigerate until servingtime. Yield: one 9-inch pie.

CARIBBEAN FUDGE PIE

¼ cup butter or margarine
¾ cup firmly packed brown sugar
3 eggs
1 (12-ounce) package semisweet chocolate morsels, melted
2 teaspoons instant coffee powder
1 teaspoon rum extract
¼ cup all-purpose flour
1½ cups chopped pecans, divided
1 unbaked 9-inch pastry shell
Whipped cream (optional)

Cream butter and sugar; add eggs, one at a time, beating well after each addition. Add melted chocolate, coffee powder, and rum extract. Stir in flour and 1 cup pecans. Pour into pastry shell; sprinkle with remaining pecans.

Bake at 375° for 25 minutes or until done. Cool; top with whipped cream, if desired. Yield: one 9-inch pie.

LEMON CHESS PIE

1 cup sugar
1 tablespoon butter or margarine, softened
Grated rind and juice of 1 lemon
¼ teaspoon salt
3 eggs, separated
1 unbaked 9-inch pastry shell

Combine sugar and butter; beat well. Add lemon rind and juice, salt, and egg yolks; beat well. Beat egg whites until light and fluffy; fold into sugar mixture. Pour filling into pastry shell; bake at 450° for 10 minutes. Reduce temperature to 350°, and bake an additional 30 minutes. Let cool before serving. Yield: one 9-inch pie.

Kids in the Kitchen

ORANGE-COCONUT BALLS

1 (12-ounce) package vanilla wafers
1 (16-ounce) package powdered sugar
½ cup margarine, softened
1 (6-ounce) can frozen orange juice
    concentrate, thawed and undiluted
1 cup finely chopped pecans or walnuts
1 (7-ounce) can flaked coconut

Crush vanilla wafers to fine crumbs; add next 4 ingredients, mixing well. Form into balls, and roll each in flaked coconut; freeze. Serve frozen. Yield: about 4 dozen.

CARAMEL CORN

2 cups firmly packed brown sugar
1 cup butter or margarine
½ cup light corn syrup
2 teaspoons salt
1 teaspoon soda
1 cup peanuts or pecans
7½ quarts popped corn

Combine brown sugar, butter, syrup, and salt in a saucepan. Bring to a boil; boil 5 minutes. Beat in soda vigorously. Stir in peanuts. Place corn in a large shallow pan. Pour sugar mixture over corn; stir. Bake at 200° for one hour, stirring every 15 minutes. Yield: 7½ quarts.

HOMEMADE LOLLIPOPS

Vegetable oil
1 cup sugar
¼ cup plus 2 tablespoons light corn
    syrup
¼ cup water
½ teaspoon peppermint, cinnamon, or
    lemon extract
Paste food coloring

Brush inside surfaces of lollipop molds with oil; set aside.

Combine sugar, corn syrup, and water in a medium saucepan. Stir gently over medium heat until sugar dissolves. (Do not splash sugar on sides of pan or candy might become grainy.) Cook without stirring until mixture reaches 310° on a candy thermometer. Remove from heat, stir in desired flavoring and coloring, and immediately pour into molds. Press sticks in indentations of molds, gently twirling to embed. Cool completely; lift lollipops out of molds. Outline or highlight shapes with Royal Icing (see page 76) if desired. Let dry and immediately wrap tightly in plastic wrap. Store in a cool, dry place. To keep them unwrapped, coat with granulated sugar to keep them from absorbing moisture from the atmosphere and becoming sticky. Yield: enough to make about 8 (2-inch) lollipops.

Note: Do not double recipe. If more lollipops are desired, make two batches.

You can substitute metal cookie cutters for molds if desired. If using cookie cutters, arrange on large piece of aluminum foil. Pour hot candy mixture into oiled cutters about ⅛-inch deep and wait until candy is firm around edges but still soft in center; then lift off cutter and press sticks into candy. (If candy hardens before all sticks are inserted, you can attach them with a small amount of additional hot lollipop mixture.) Let cool completely and wrap in plastic.

Above: Decorate a wreath with lollipops made in Christmas shapes; coat them with sugar if you don't plan to wrap them.

Above left: Pour hot lollipop mixture quickly into oiled molds and insert sticks before mixture hardens; work carefully—it's hot!

Left: A basketful of lollipops can be a colorful table arrangement and a delightful way to serve them to children.

Children around your house will eagerly lend a hand at pulling Old-Fashioned Taffy; it's funniest when it pulls apart. On hutch, Candied Citrus Peel and Stained-Glass Windows.

CANDIED CITRUS PEEL

   1 **thick-skinned grapefruit**
   2 **thick-skinned oranges**
   1 **thick-skinned lemon**
1½ **cups sugar**
      Additional sugar

Peel fruits. Cut peel into 2- × ¼-inch strips. Cover with cold water in a saucepan, and let come to a boil. Drain and repeat three times. Drain; add 1½ cups sugar. Cook over low heat, stirring until sugar dissolves. Continue to cook until peel becomes transparent and has absorbed all the syrup. Roll each piece in additional sugar. Store in covered containers. Yield: 1 to 1½ cups.

OLD-FASHIONED TAFFY

2½ **cups sugar**
 ½ **cup water**
 ¼ **cup vinegar**
 ⅛ **teaspoon salt**
  1 **tablespoon butter or margarine**
  1 **teaspoon vanilla extract**

Combine first 5 ingredients in a small Dutch oven; cook, without stirring, over medium heat just until mixture reaches soft crack stage (270°). Remove from heat. Stir in vanilla.

Pour candy onto a well-buttered 15- × 10- × 1-inch jellyroll pan or slab of marble. Let cool to touch; pull candy until light in color and difficult to pull. (Butter hands if candy is sticky.) Divide candy in half, and pull into a rope, 1 inch in diameter. Cut taffy into 1-inch pieces; wrap each piece individually in waxed paper. Yield: about 40 (1-inch) pieces.

Save candymaking steps like cooking and chopping ingredients for older folks, but children can lend a hand at shaping Festive Mints.

STAINED-GLASS WINDOWS

   1 **(12-ounce) package chocolate morsels**
  ½ **cup butter or margarine**
   1 **(10½-ounce) package fruit-flavored or
      regular miniature marshmallows**
   1 **cup finely chopped pecans or walnuts
     Flaked coconut**

Melt chocolate and butter over low heat; cool.
Add marshmallows and pecans to chocolate
mixture. Shape into 2 rolls 1½ to 2 inches in
diameter; roll each in coconut. Refrigerate.

   When rolls are thoroughly chilled, slice into
½-inch slices. Yield: about 3 dozen.

FESTIVE MINTS

   1 **(16-ounce) package powdered sugar**
  ½ **cup margarine, softened**
   2 **tablespoons evaporated milk**
   4 **to 5 drops of peppermint flavoring
     Few drops of desired food coloring**

Combine all ingredients in a large mixing bowl.
Beat at high speed of electric mixer until well
blended; then knead until smooth.

   Shape mints in rubber candy molds, and place
on paper towel-covered baking sheets. Cover
with another paper towel, and let stand overnight to harden. Yield: 8½ to 9 dozen mints.

Party & Gift Ideas

SWEET AND SPICY MUSTARD

¼ cup plus 1 tablespoon dry mustard
½ cup sugar
1 tablespoon all-purpose flour
½ teaspoon salt
  Dash of red pepper
2 eggs, beaten
½ cup vinegar
1 tablespoon butter or margarine

Combine mustard, sugar, flour, salt, and red pepper in top of a double boiler. Add eggs and vinegar, blending thoroughly. Place over boiling water; cook, stirring constantly, until thickened. Add butter; stir until melted. Cool mixture; then store in a jar in the refrigerator. Yield: 1⅓ cups.

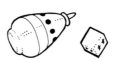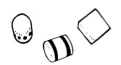

QUICK APRICOT MARMALADE

2 (6-ounce) packages dried apricots, finely chopped
1 cup sugar
1 (15¼-ounce) can crushed pineapple, undrained

Combine apricots and sugar; add water to barely cover. Cook over medium heat 15 minutes, stirring frequently. Add pineapple; cook 5 minutes, stirring frequently. Spoon into hot sterilized jars, leaving ¼-inch headspace. Cover at once with metal lids, and screw bands tight. Process in boiling-water bath 10 minutes. Yield: 4 half pints.

HOLIDAY RELISH

4 cups whole raw cranberries, ground
2 apples, washed, cored, and finely chopped
  Juice of 2 oranges
1 (8-ounce) can crushed pineapple
1 cup chopped pecans
2¾ cups sugar

Combine all ingredients, mixing well. Cover and refrigerate overnight. Yield: about 2 quarts.

PARTY O'S

4 cups toasted oat cereal
2 cups pretzel sticks
1 cup pecans or walnuts
¼ cup butter or margarine, melted
1 tablespoon Worcestershire sauce
1 teaspoon paprika
½ teaspoon garlic salt

Combine cereal, pretzel sticks, and pecans in an ungreased 13- × 9- × 2-inch baking pan. Combine butter, Worcestershire sauce, paprika, and garlic salt; pour over cereal mixture, tossing until well coated.

Bake at 275° for 30 minutes; stir occasionally. Store in airtight container. Yield: 6 cups.

CURRIED CASHEWS

¼ cup butter or margarine
2 cups cashews
1 to 2 tablespoons curry powder
  Salt to taste

Melt butter in a skillet; add cashews. Cook over low heat until nuts are browned, stirring frequently. Drain on absorbent towels. Sprinkle with curry powder and salt. Yield: 2 cups.

Festive Cheese Ball is a garlic-flavored blend of three kinds of cheese.

CHEESE WAFERS

  1 cup all-purpose flour
  ½ teaspoon salt
  ¾ cup chopped pecans or walnuts
  2 cups (8 ounces) shredded Cheddar
    cheese
  ½ cup butter or margarine, softened

Combine flour, salt, pecans, and cheese in a mixing bowl; add butter and beat well. Divide dough in half; shape each half into a 10-inch roll. Wrap in waxed paper and chill at least 2 hours.

Slice rolls into ¼-inch slices and place on greased cookie sheets. Bake at 350° for 15 minutes. Yield: about 6 dozen.

Note: Rolls can be prepared ahead of time and frozen. Soften at room temperature for 1½ hours, slice, and bake as directed.

FESTIVE CHEESE BALL

  1 (16-ounce) package process cheese
    spread, softened
  1 pound sharp Cheddar cheese,
    softened
  1 (8-ounce) package cream cheese,
    softened
  4 cloves garlic, minced
  ½ cup chopped pecans or walnuts
    Chopped pecans or walnuts, or
    paprika and minced parsley

Combine cheese, mixing until well blended. Stir in garlic and ½ cup chopped pecans. Divide mixture into 3 equal portions, and shape into balls. Roll each ball in nuts or in paprika and parsley. Yield: 3 (1½-cup) cheese balls.

Add a festive touch to your party by serving Dill Dip from a wreath of fresh vegetables.

VEGETABLE WREATH

2 to 3 carrots
1 turnip
15 radishes
1 bunch celery
1 bunch green onions
1 bunch broccoli
1 head cauliflower
1 pint cherry tomatoes
1 to 2 bunches fresh parsley

Wash vegetables, and drain well. Slice carrots and turnip into ⅛-inch slices. Cut about three-fourths of slices into flower shapes, using a canapé cutter. Cut remaining slices into ¼-inch circles, using kitchen shears. Match carrot flowers to turnip circles, and turnip flowers to carrot circles; insert toothpick just through flower and almost through circle. Place flowers in a bowl of ice water and refrigerate until needed.

Prepare vegetables ahead of time and refrigerate until assembling wreath. Gather all utensils needed.

After washing parsley and trimming stems, tack sprigs to the plastic foam circle with florist's picks, overlapping the sprigs to ensure complete coverage.

Skewer vegetables with toothpicks and stick them into wreath.

Trim stem ends from radishes. Cut radishes, using a commercial radish rose cutter, or slice petals in radishes with a sharp paring knife, following pattern of roses in photos. Place in a bowl of ice water and refrigerate for petals to open.

Cut celery stalks into 2-inch pieces. Cut several slits at both ends of each piece, cutting almost to the center. Place in a bowl of ice water and refrigerate for ends to curl.

Trim both ends of green onions, leaving about 2 inches of green tops. Place green onions on a cutting board. Using a sharp knife, cut through length of green tops in several places. Place in bowl of ice water and refrigerate for tops to curl.

Trim flowerets from broccoli and cauliflower. Place broccoli and cauliflower flowerets and cherry tomatoes in separate plastic bags and refrigerate until ready to assemble wreath.

Wash parsley thoroughly and drain well. Trim stem ends from parsley. Attach parsley to the plastic-foam circle, using florist's picks and overlapping sprigs to ensure complete coverage.

Skewer vegetables with toothpicks and stick them into wreath. Celery fans and tomatoes are easier to attach by inserting the toothpick in the wreath first, then sticking the vegetable onto the end of the pick. Serve dip from bowl placed in center of wreath.

DILL DIP

⅔ cup commercial sour cream
⅔ cup mayonnaise
1 tablespoon finely chopped fresh parsley
1 tablespoon instant minced onion
1 tablespoon dried dillweed
¼ teaspoon dry mustard

Combine all ingredients; mix well. Chill before serving. Yield: about 1½ cups.

You can make specially flavored vinegars using either fresh or dried herbs; standing time allows the flavors to mellow.

HERB VINEGARS

Cut desired herbs and reserve a few sprigs of each variety. Loosely fill large jars with fresh herbs, bruising herbs slightly to release maximum flavor. (If you use dried herbs, measure ¼ to ½ cup for each quart of vinegar.) Cover herbs with vinegar and seal the jars.

The steeping time varies, depending on how you process the vinegars. If you do not warm the vinegar, it must steep for 1 to 2 months. You can speed the process, however, with heat from the sun or from your range top.

Solar Vinegars: Put jars of fresh herbs and vinegar outside for 2 weeks. Taste for strength, and when the flavor is transferred to the vinegar, continue the steps below.

Range Top Method: Bring vinegar almost to a boil before pouring it over bruised herbs in jars. Do not boil the vinegar as that can decay the herbs and ruin the flavor. When processed with warm vinegar, herb vinegars will be ready for tasting in 6 to 10 days.

Remove herbs from the jars and strain the vinegar through cheesecloth into decorative bottles. Add a fresh sprig of the appropriate herb to each bottle for decoration and identification.

Single Herb Vinegars

Tarragon: The gourmet's classic flavoring, tarragon vinegar is best when made with white wine vinegar.

Mint: Steep in cider vinegar for use in an English-style lamb sauce or on a fresh fruit salad.

Dill: Steep in cider vinegar and save for pickling brine.

Lavender blossoms: Lavender blossoms steeped in distilled white or white wine vinegar will give a pale lavender color. Versatile lavender vinegar adds tartness to a fruit salad.

Chive blossoms: Process these blossoms in distilled white or white wine vinegar for a multipurpose vinegar with a delicate pink color.

Dark opal basil: These purple leaves will turn distilled white vinegar or white wine vinegar dark red.

Nasturtium: Use only a few nasturtium flowers in white vinegar because the color will leach quickly. The peppery flavor that adds such zest to summer salads can do the same to green winter salads or marinades.

Combination Vinegars

Eleven-herb vinegar: Use roughly equal amounts of fresh parsley, thyme, mint, burnet, basil, marjoram, lemon balm, rosemary, oregano, chives, and dill in white wine vinegar.

Garlic-tarragon: Put four peeled garlic buds, a handful of whole cloves, and loosely packed tarragon in a 1-gallon jug of cider vinegar.

Lemon: Lemon balm, lemon verbena, and a long, curled piece of lemon peel in distilled white vinegar make a tart vinegar for fruit and green salads.

Joys of Giving

Christmas is the happiest time of the year—filled with thoughts of home and family, food and friends, and especially with finding the perfect gifts for the ones you love. Often, though, the season brings such a flurry of activity that instead of spending time leisurely searching for the right gifts, holiday shoppers find themselves caught at the last minute, fighting crowds and traffic, in a frantic race with time.

This year make shopping easier and more fun. Let *Southern Living Marketplace* help you shop by mail. We have collected the very best gift ideas and decorations for the Christmas season—all chosen to suit *Southern Living* tastes and lifestyles.

Yummy foods you won't find in any store, extra special decorations for your home, exciting new ornaments to add to your collection, china and linens for festive entertaining, plus dozens of other warm and wonderful gift ideas to make

shopping ever so much easier. Your family and friends will cherish the gifts you choose, and this easy way of shopping will mean that you'll have more time to spend enjoying the holidays!

Our expert staff will handle your order with the care it deserves, making sure that it arrives in good condition and on time. We'll even handle gift wrapping and write a special personal message on the card if you desire. Let *Southern Living Marketplace* share a little bit of the Christmas spirit with you by helping you with your shopping. We'll do a good job . . . because that's our special Christmas gift to you. Happy Holidays!

Special Trimmings

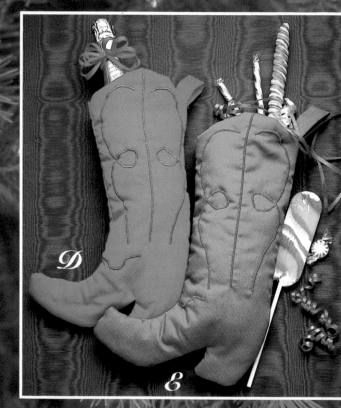

F

G

H

A A pair of familiar faces. Porcelain bisque clip-on cardinal ornaments from Gorham. Cheery for tree or wreath. 3½" long. Set of 2.
#2X115A, Cardinal Ornaments, $10.50

B Tree top nest, a very different way to give your tree the feeling of outdoors. Raffia, branches, ribbons and a pair of tiny finches give it a gentle charm that is hard to match.
#2X115B, Tree Top Nest, $25.00

C Everlasting beauty, our hand-painted metal wreath, designed especially for us! Handsome indoors or out. Approx. 10" diam.
#2X115C, Poinsettia Wreath, $49.50

D E Go West for Christmas with our cowboy boot stockings in red or green polyester and cotton. Hang by the fire or give one as a gift filled with a bottle of his favorite spirits.
#2X115D, Red Cowboy Boot, $10.00
#2X115E, Green Cowboy Boot, $10.00

F Deck the halls with our unusual twig decoration with tartan ribbons, tiny fabric flowers and bright, lacquered cherries. Handmade just for us, it can be used over a door, window, mirror or mantel, or as a centerpiece with candlesticks. Approx. 36" long. (Sorry, no gift box.)
#2X115F, Twig Decoration, $29.50

G Hand-painted wooden weathervane ornaments, a touch of country for your tree. Set of 6 includes 5 animals and 1 angel. 5" high.
#2X115G, Weathervane Set, $19.00

H Standing, or hanging on your tree, this pair of country bears will add to your Christmas cheer. Hand painted and exquisitely dressed, they're great collectibles. 6½" high. Set of 2.
#2X115H, Country Bears, $29.00

A If you've never tried Popcrackle, you're missing a treat! Popcorn, almonds, pecans and peanuts, smothered in a buttery-rich honey-vanilla glaze. 2 lbs. packed in a holiday green gift tin.
#2X116A, Popcrackle, $13.50

B Georgia's own peanuts, roasted, then glazed with a scrumptious sugar coating. Packed in a bright blue tin bucket to keep them fresh! 3 lbs.
#2X116B, Sugared Peanuts, $15.00

C A traditional favorite, jumbo Southern pecan halves, slow-roasted and lightly salted, then packed in a Christmas red, reusable tin. 2½ lbs. of delicious snacking.
#2X116C, Salted Pecans, $25.00

D Catch the cookie express and make one of the most delightful decorations we've seen. Kit includes prebaked gingerbread cookie shapes that slot together with support of Royal Icing (recipe included), pastry bag, tip, and decorative candies. Make a family project of creating this Christmas choo-choo! Will last from year to year. Assembled, it measures almost 2 feet long!
#2X116D, Cookie Train Kit, $24.50

E So much a part of a Southern family Christmas, shining jars full of homemade treats. Set of 3 clear heavy glass jars with old-fashioned domed lids, 8¼", 10", and 11½" high,

dishwasher safe. Fill them to overflowing for a clearly wonderful present!
#2X117E, The Jars, $19.50

F Sunday Dinner Biscuits with country butters. 3 lb. calico sack of Arkansas' War Eagle Mill special whole wheat biscuit mix with added wheat germ, plus a pint Mason jar of open kettle apple butter with honey, and one of smooth-spreading pumpkin butter. A Down-Home Treat!
#2X117F, Biscuits & Butters, $14.00

G To give homemade treats a special air of thoughtfulness, pack them in our holiday gift tins, with foil liners for baking. Set includes four nostalgic Christmas designs and four liners. Each keeps approx. 1 lb. of goodies fresh and tempting.
#2X117G, Holiday Tins/Liners, $13.50

H A mouth-watering Southern favorite, pickled Vidalia onions, is teamed with a simply delicious onion relish. Serve both on crackers with cream cheese and draw raves. Made from an old Georgia recipe. Two 16-oz. jars.
#2X117H, Onions/Relish, $12.50

J Who else but Southern Living? Our own bright red apron tells everyone "I (love) Southern Living Recipes!" The same apron is worn by our test kitchen and cooking school staffs. Hand-screened on poly/cotton duck. No iron, one size fits all good cooks!
#2X117J, Recipe Lover's Apron, $14.00

K It's been a tradition in Tennessee since antebellum times to serve homemade, chocolate-covered Bourbon Balls. Our special candy, ultra-creamy, bourbon-pecan centers coated in deep dark chocolate, comes packed in a delightful Santa tin. No preservatives, so open immediately and indulge. The sweetest gift! 2 lbs.
#2X117K, Bourbon Balls/Tin, $22.50

A

B

Glorious Gifts

C

D

E

A Christmas is coming, and fat geese are right in style. Our Country Goose place mats with tartan napkin kerchiefs are no-iron poly/cotton. Set of four mats and four napkins.
#2X119A, Goose Mats/Napkins, $27.50

B "Plant" your poinsettia in our hand-painted bamboo basket. Approx. 10" x 11½" wide, each is signed by the artist and no two are exactly alike. A Southern Living Marketplace Exclusive!
#2X119B, Poinsettia Basket, $31.50

C Fond memories of each Santa Season can be treasured for years in this jolly red calico album, complete with 5" x 7" frame on the front. The 12"-square album (takes standard refills) comes with a tag giving the name and age of the senior artisan who made it.
#2X119C, Family Album, $26.00

D Bachelor Button Chili Pot! Hand-painted glazed stoneware with lid and ladle. Holds 4 quarts, is oven, freezer and dishwasher safe.
#2X119D, Chili Pot/Ladle, $73.50

E To match our chili pot, a set of 4 oversized cups. Perfect for chili, soup or ice cream.
#2X119E, Chili Cups, $33.50

F Santa's Bake Shop apron adds fun to Christmas cooking for the 4- to 9-year-old gourmet. Red cotton with calico trim and vinyl backing and in the pocket, Santa's favorite cookie recipe, mixing spoon and Santa cookie cutter.
#2X119F, Bake Shop Apron, $16.50

G Kitchen fun for children, two never-fail cooking kits. Chocolate Taffy Pull Kit, just pull to make over 100 pieces. Little Red Hen Bread Maker Kit with pans, mix, honey, and coloring book. Just add water to make delicious yeast bread.
#2X119G, Taffy Pull/Bread Kit, $16.50

H Christmas countdown in gingerbread, a pretty decoration with a treat for each day from Dec. 1 to 23, and a BIG cookie for Christmas Eve.
#2X119H, Gingerbread Calendar, $14.00

J Apple head doll—a collector's treasure! You'll love our Pastry Peddler Doll with her basket full of real breads and rolls. Handmade, and no two are exactly alike. 15" high.
#2X119J, Apple Head Doll, $75.00

A

B

A Reflections in brass, classic shell sconces that say so much about your good taste. Beautifully designed for stunning lighting in any room. The pair, approx. 12" high, candles not included.
#2X120A, Shell Sconces, $52.00

B Reproduction Mason decoy box, hand carved from pine, finished to a hand-rubbed glow. The box, with an authentic brass shotgun shell and a lift-off lid, comes in a reusable wooden gift crate. An impressive desk top trophy for home or executive office. 13" x 7" x 9½" high.
#2X120B, Mallard Box, $99.50

C A bubbling kettle says an old-fashioned "Welcome," and ours does lots of bubbling because it holds 5 quarts. Solid copper beauty, tin lined, a decorative, practical, and traditional accent for any Southern home.
#2X120C, Copper Kettle, $49.50

D Give your whole house the warm and friendly scent of Christmas with our Merry Christmas Boil Bags. Simply simmer in water while the aroma of spices fills the air. Can be cooled and reused many times. Set of 3.
#2X120D, Boil Bags, $10.00

E Angelic attraction, our delightful angel wall shelf, taken from an English wood carving (circa 1840). Handcast, with an antiqued walnut finish, it's an elegant bit of whimsy for your home.
#2X120E, Angel Shelf, $28.50

F Gabriel heralds the season on our charming terra cotta mold, attractive displayed on a wall. The glazed interior makes it perfect for oven or refrigerator. 8" x 11".
#2X120F, Angel Mold, $16.00

G A natural symbol of the holidays, pine cones bleached to the shade of pale wood are stunning heaped in a basket or hung on the tree. Bag of 10 large cones.
#2X120G, Bleached Pine Cones, $12.50

HJ Patchwork for Christmas, big old-fashioned stockings made from antique quilts. Stockings will vary. 17" high, for either boys or girls.
#2X120H, Boy's Stocking, $23.00
#2X120J, Girl's Stocking, $23.00

C

D

E

F

G

H

I

A

A Wonderfully fragrant Williamsburg spice wreath, a colonial inspiration that will last forever. Entirely handmade on a straw base, it features aromatic lavendar, cinnamon sticks, allspice, star anise, potpourri and dried rose petals. Approx. 15" diam.

#2X122A, Williamsburg Wreath, $42.00

B Hello, Dollies! Charming little Victorian ladies with delicate hand-painted porcelain faces, hands and feet. Dressed in pastels, they'll grace any doll collection, decorate holiday packages, or hang as ornaments on your tree. Each 8" Gorham doll is different; please let us choose one for you to love.

#2X122B, Porcelain Dolls, $10.50

Southern Living MARKETPLACE

Department CA
P.O. Box 1425
Alexandria, VA 22313

ORDERING INFORMATION
FOR ITEMS ON PAGES 114-122

Telephone Orders: For your convenience, you may order through our 24-hour, 7-days-a-week, TOLL-FREE telephone. Dial 800-323-1717 and ask for Operator 144. (Illinois residents dial 800-942-8881.) Please have this book and your credit card handy.

Mail Orders: Copy the line that includes the order number, name, and price from the bottom of each description. Total your order (Alabama residents add 4% sales tax). Then add the correct amount for shipping and handling from the chart below. Enclose a check or money order for this amount and mail to the address above.

Bank Card Orders: To charge your order, please include the following information: 1) bank card type (VISA, MasterCard, or American Express), 2) bank card number, 3) expiration date, 4) signature as it appears on your card.

Customer Service: For inquiries about your order, call 703-960-7833 9-5 EST (sorry, no collect calls to this number).

GIFT WRAPPING: Please indicate clearly on your order and add $2.00 for each item you wish presented in our beautiful gift box with an embossed gold card. If desired, include a brief message to be written on the gift card.

SHIPPING: All orders are shipped UPS so please include your street address and house or apartment number with each order. If you wish any item to be sent to an address other than your own, please specify on your order.

SHIPPING & HANDLING

If your order totals:	Add
Up to $15.00	$2.00
$15.01 to $30.00	$3.25
$30.01 to $50.00	$4.50
$50.01 or more	$5.00

Southern Living Marketplace values you as a customer and is confident of the quality of our gift items. We, therefore, unconditionally guarantee all of our products. If you are dissatisfied, simply return the item for a prompt exchange. No COD packages, please. Only orders received before December 1 will arrive in time for Christmas, and only limited quantities are available for some items, so ORDER EARLY!

B

122

Christmas Journal

Christmas is the season of imagination and sharing, and each of us finds our own way of enjoying the season. By the way we choose our guests, our foods, our trees, our gifts, our parties—all the elements of our individual celebrations—we tailor the holiday to our own needs and desires. Christmas is best, however, when it is planned and completed without too much confusion—forgetting an important gift or showing up at 8:00 for a dinner party that was scheduled for 6:00.

Christmas Journal helps with the planning and arrangement of your holiday activities and organizes an otherwise hectic season. A Card List is a handy key to your success in this sharing of friendship and good wishes. Encourage your family members to add to the list as they think of people who should be remembered; a check in the "sent" column will indicate your progress in completing the list. Size Charts can be a help to the entire family. A chart for each member will allow others

to choose gifts that will fit—without divulging the idea by asking a size. Gifts & Wishes has two uses. The list can be a simple record of gifts purchased. An alternate use (particularly if the whole family will read the book and discover your secrets) is as a wish list in which family members can leave broad hints about the gifts they would like to receive. A Holiday Calendar for November and December will help with scheduling all the activities of the season. Encourage family members to add to the calendar as early as possible so that you can resolve conflicts and make necessary preparations.

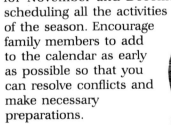

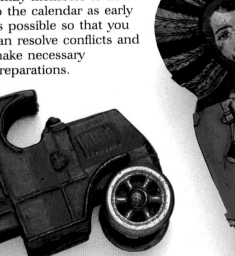

Mailing

CARDS

As you are planning your Christmas cards, keep in mind the following regulations by the U.S. Postal Service. All envelopes must be rectangular in shape. Cards and envelopes smaller than 3½" × 5" cannot be mailed. Envelopes larger than 6⅛" × 11½", even if they weigh less than 1 ounce, require extra postage.

PACKAGES

Packages may be sent through the U.S. Postal Service by parcel post in weights up to 40 pounds (70 pounds for rural routes and small towns) and measurements of 84" of combined length and girth. "Priority" and "Express Mail" (at higher prices) can be used for packages up to 70 pounds in weight and up to 100" in combined length and girth. Refer to the chart for requirements of packaging, closing, and addressing.

United Parcel Service (UPS) accepts packages up to 50 pounds and up to 108" in combined length and girth. There is a pick-up fee for door-to-door service, but in peak periods, you may find it more convenient to take the package to UPS customer service.

CATEGORY	EXAMPLES	CONTAINER	CUSHIONING	CLOSURE
Soft Goods		Self-supporting box or tear-resistant bag		Reinforced tape or sealed bag
Liquids		Leak proof interior and secondary containers	Absorbent	Sealed with filament tape
Powders		Must be sift-proof		Sealed with filament tape
Perishables		Impermeable to content odor	Absorbent	Sealed with filament tape
Fragile Items		Fiberboard (minimum 175 lb test)	To distribute shocks and separate from container surfaces with foamed plastic or padding	Sealed and reinforced with filament tape
Awkward Loads		Fiberboard tubes and boxes with length not over 10 times girth	Pre-formed fiberboard or foamed plastic shapes	Tube ends equal to side wall strength

CONTAINER

Fiberboard

Manufacturer's Certificate

125 lb test to 20 lbs
175 lb test to 40 lbs
275 lb test to 70 lbs

Paperboard up to 10 lbs

CUSHIONING

Wrap each item individually with enough padding to prevent damage from shock

Separate wrapped items from outer package surfaces with padding or foamed plastic

CLOSURE

Pressure Sensitive Filament Tape is preferable to prevent accidental opening

Reinforced Kraft Paper Tape

Kraft Paper Tape

ADDRESSING

Address Labels should be readable from 30" away and should not be easily smeared or washed off

Should contain ZIP Code

Return Address should also be included inside of carton

Adapted from a U.S. Postal Service poster.

Christmas Card List

Name	rec'd	sent

Name	rec'd	sent

CHRISTMAS CARD LIST (CONTINUED)

Name	rec'd	sent

Name	rec'd	sent

CHRISTMAS CARD LIST (CONTINUED)

Name	rec'd	sent

Name	rec'd	sent

Gifts & Wishes

Name _____

_____

_____

_____

Name _____

_____

_____

_____

Name _____

_____

_____

_____

Name _____

_____

_____

_____

Name _____

_____

_____

_____

Name _____

_____

_____

_____

Name _____

_____

_____

_____

Name _____

_____

_____

_____

Size Charts

Name

_____

_____

_____

Name

_____

_____

_____

Name

_____

_____

_____

Name

_____

_____

_____

Name		Name	
height	weight	height	weight
coat	slacks	coat	slacks
dress	pajamas	dress	pajamas
suit	bathrobe	suit	bathrobe
sweater	shoes	sweater	shoes
shirt	hat	shirt	hat
blouse	gloves	blouse	gloves
skirt	ring	skirt	ring

Name		Name	
height	weight	height	weight
coat	slacks	coat	slacks
dress	pajamas	dress	pajamas
suit	bathrobe	suit	bathrobe
sweater	shoes	sweater	shoes
shirt	hat	shirt	hat
blouse	gloves	blouse	gloves
skirt	ring	skirt	ring

Name		Name	
height	weight	height	weight
coat	slacks	coat	slacks
dress	pajamas	dress	pajamas
suit	bathrobe	suit	bathrobe
sweater	shoes	sweater	shoes
shirt	hat	shirt	hat
blouse	gloves	blouse	gloves
skirt	ring	skirt	ring

Holiday Calendar

Monday, November 1

Tuesday, November 2

Wednesday, November 3

Thursday, November 4

Friday, November 5

Saturday, November 6

Sunday, November 7

Monday, November 8

Tuesday, November 9

Wednesday, November 10

Thursday, November 11

Friday, November 12

Saturday, November 13

Sunday, November 14

Sunday, November 21

Monday, November 15

Monday, November 22

Tuesday, November 16

Tuesday, November 23

Wednesday, November 17

Wednesday, November 24

Thursday, November 18

Thursday, November 25   *Thanksgiving*

Friday, November 19

Friday, November 26

Saturday, November 20

Saturday, November 27

Sunday, November 28

Sunday, December 5

Monday, November 29

Monday, December 6

Tuesday, November 30

Tuesday, December 7

Wednesday, December 1

Wednesday, December 8

Thursday, December 2

Thursday, December 9

Friday, December 3

Friday, December 10

Saturday, December 4

Saturday, December 11

Sunday, December 12

_____

Monday, December 13

_____

Tuesday, December 14

_____

Wednesday, December 15

_____

Thursday, December 16

_____

Friday, December 17

_____

Saturday, December 18

Sunday, December 19

_____

Monday, December 20

_____

Tuesday, December 21

_____

Wednesday, December 22

_____

Thursday, December 23

_____

Friday, December 24

_____

Saturday, December 25   Christmas

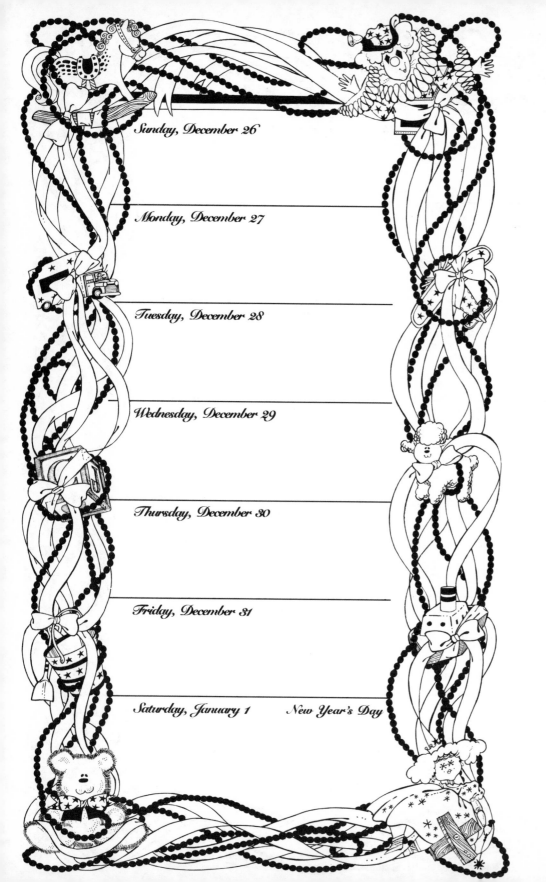

Sunday, December 26

Monday, December 27

Tuesday, December 28

Wednesday, December 29

Thursday, December 30

Friday, December 31

Saturday, January 1   New Year's Day

Baker's Ornaments

Directions on page 64

Full size pattern

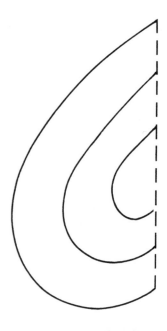

Patterns

Luminaries

Directions on page 25

Full size pattern

Trace inside (heavy) line
for cutout on sack

Trace outside (lighter) line
for tissue paper star

Christmas Cardinals

Directions on page 46
Full size pattern

Staple here

Slit for wing

A Quiet Celebration

Directions on page 35

Full size pattern
Wing for angel

LUMINARIES
Directions on page 25

Full size pattern
Half of design

Trace inside (heavy) line
for cutout on sack

Trace outside (lighter) line
for tissue paper tree

Place on fold

136

Full size pattern
Half of design

Trace heavy line for cutout on sack
Trace outside line for tissue paper angel
Trace keyhole line for white angel face and dress

Patchwork Wreaths

Point A

Side A

Side A

Directions on page 65
Finished size
Add seam allowances

Holly Place Mats

Directions on page 58

Napkin ring

Cut 2 for each
Full size pattern

Ribbon

Scrolls & Ribbons

Directions on page 43

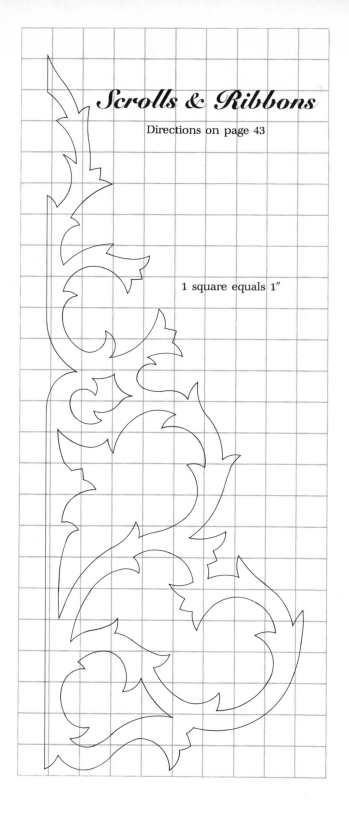

1 square equals 1"

Partridges & Pears

Directions on page 50

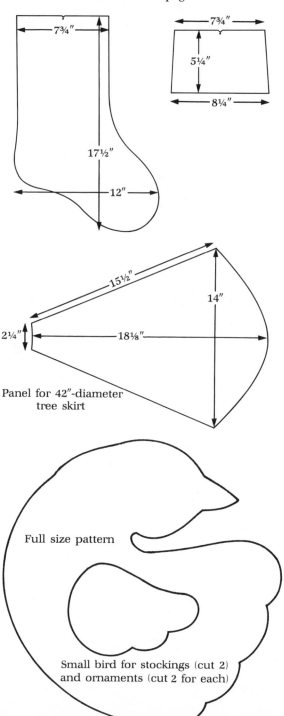

7¾"

7¾"

5¼"

8¼"

17½"

12"

15½"

14"

2¼"

18⅛"

Panel for 42"-diameter tree skirt

Full size pattern

Small bird for stockings (cut 2) and ornaments (cut 2 for each)

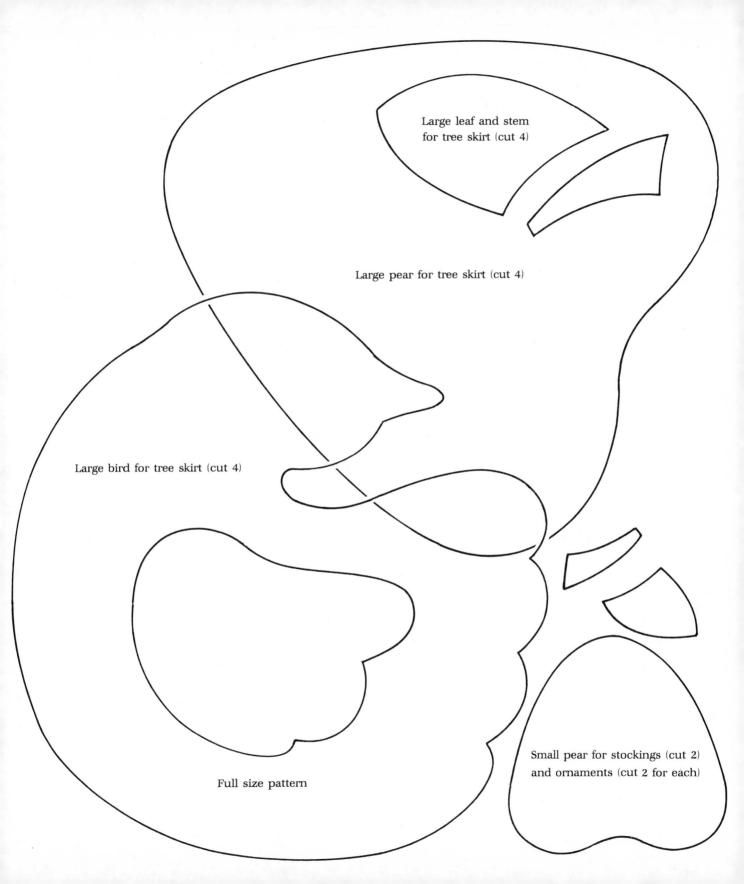

Large leaf and stem
for tree skirt (cut 4)

Large pear for tree skirt (cut 4)

Large bird for tree skirt (cut 4)

Full size pattern

Small pear for stockings (cut 2)
and ornaments (cut 2 for each)

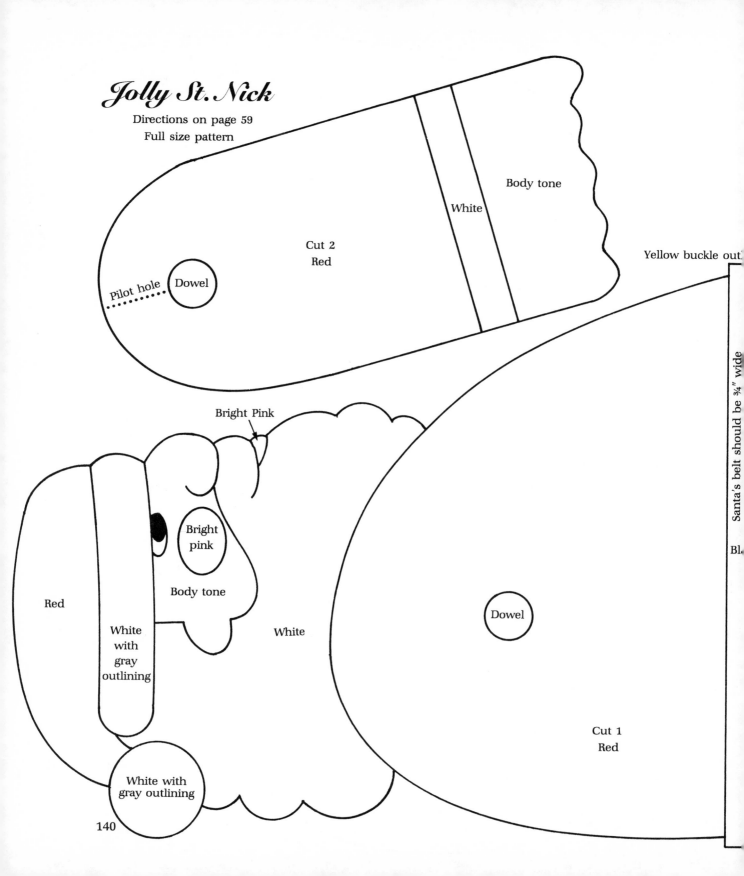

Jolly St. Nick

Directions on page 59
Full size pattern

Body tone

White

Cut 2
Red

Pilot hole · · · · · · · · · · Dowel

Yellow buckle out

Bright Pink

Bright pink

Santa's belt should be ¾" wide

Bl.

Red

Body tone

White
with
gray
outlining

White

Dowel

White with
gray outlining

Cut 1
Red

140

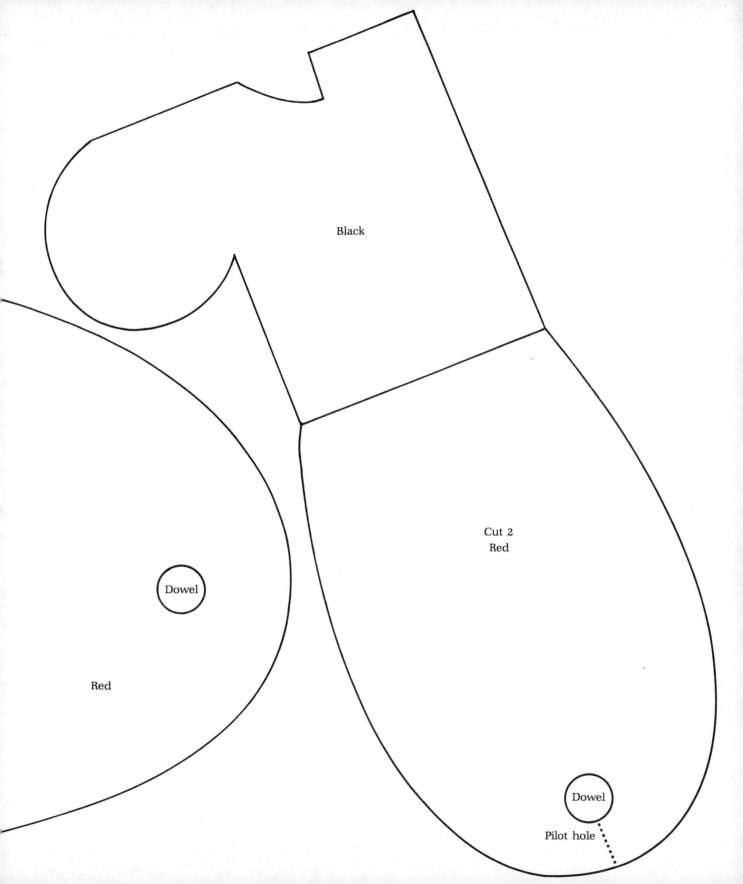

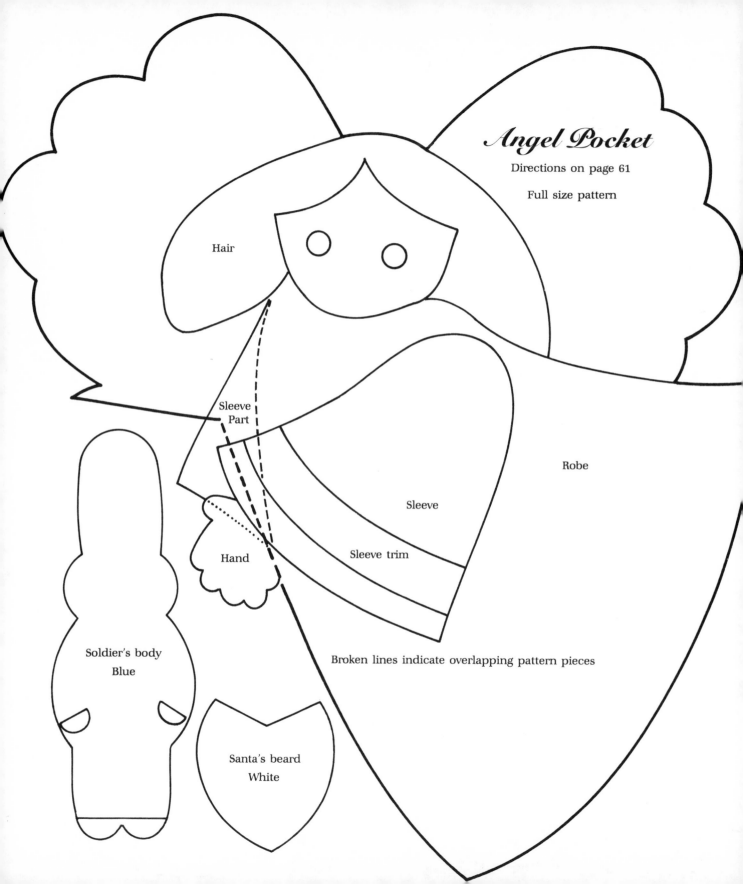

Angel Pocket

Directions on page 61

Full size pattern

Hair

Sleeve Part

Robe

Sleeve

Hand

Sleeve trim

Soldier's body
Blue

Broken lines indicate overlapping pattern pieces

Santa's beard
White

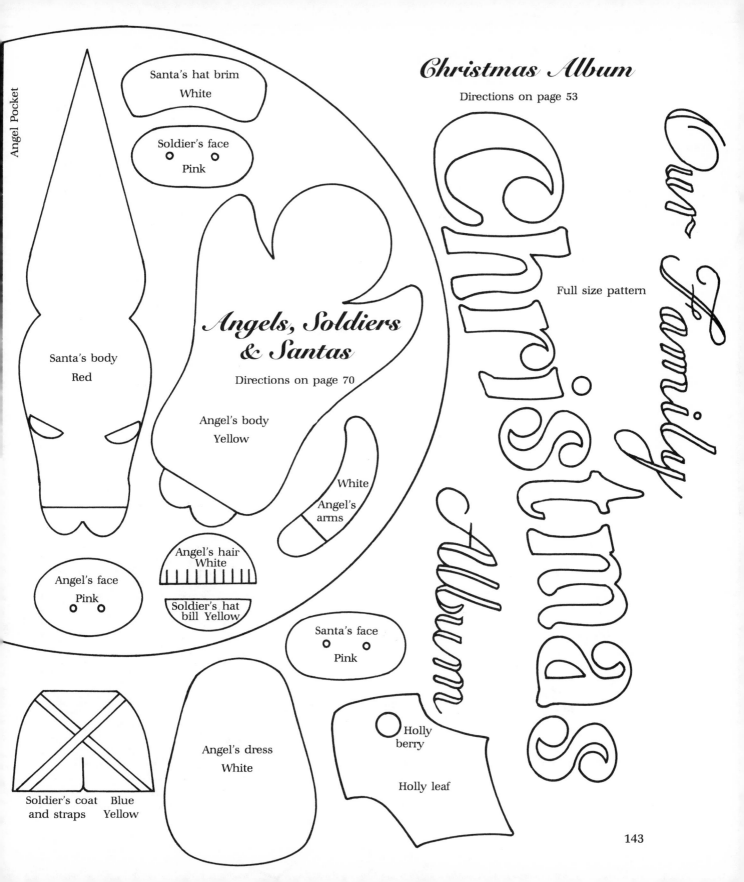

Angel Pocket

Santa's hat brim
White

Soldier's face
Pink

Christmas Album

Directions on page 53

Our Family

Christmas Album

Full size pattern

*Angels, Soldiers
& Santas*

Directions on page 70

Santa's body
Red

Angel's body
Yellow

White
Angel's
arms

Angel's hair
White

Soldier's hat
bill Yellow

Angel's face
Pink

Santa's face
Pink

Soldier's coat   Blue
and straps   Yellow

Angel's dress
White

Holly
berry

Holly leaf

143

Smocked Sherbets

Directions on page 63

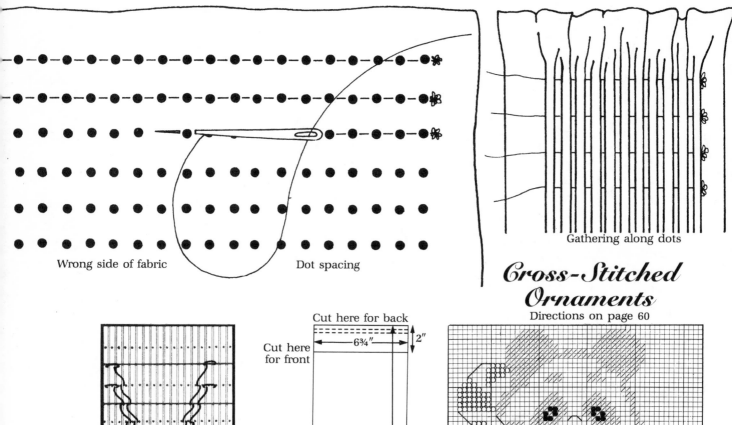

Wrong side of fabric   Dot spacing

Gathering along dots

Cross-Stitched Ornaments

Directions on page 60

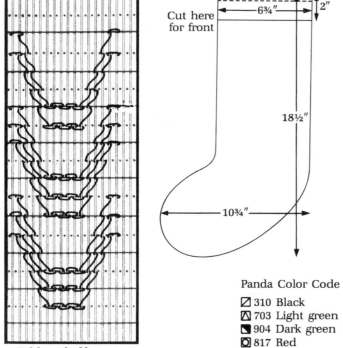

Cut here for back

Cut here for front

6¾"

2"

18½"

10¾"

★ Cable; 4 half-step waves down; 5 cables; 4 half-step waves up; repeat from ★.

Panda Color Code

☑ 310 Black
◩ 703 Light green
◪ 904 Dark green
◖ 817 Red
◕ 799 Light blue

Backstitch candy cane red, mouth and nose black, around feet and arms white, and bowtie and knot dark green.

144

Backstitch around star light blue and holly stem dark green.

Angel Color Code

- ⊠ 725 Golden yellow
- ▲ 799 Light blue
- ⊞ 444 Yellow
- ◉ 945 Flesh
- ■ 3326 Pink
- ⊿ 703 Light green
- ⊟ 904 Dark green
- ◉ 817 Red

Soldier Color Code

- ◐ 666 Red
- ◣ 792 Royal blue
- ◎ 725 Golden yellow
- ⊟ 434 Medium brown
- ⊡ 951 Flesh
- ⊿ 310 Black
- ⊠ White

Backstitch glove, arms, and epaulettes black, and belt buckle golden yellow.

Gingerbread House

Directions on page 74

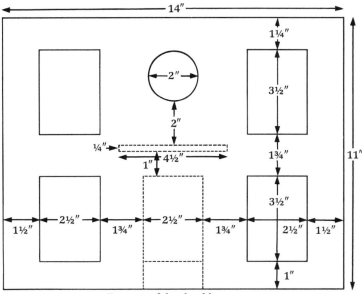

Front and back of house
Cut door and porch roof slot for front
Cut window for back

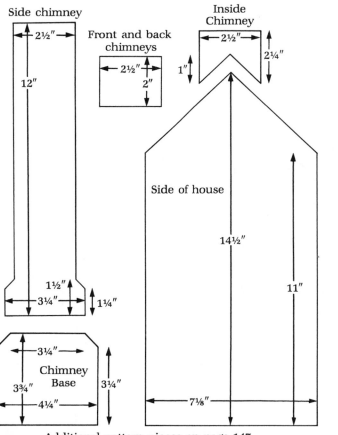

Additional pattern pieces on page 147

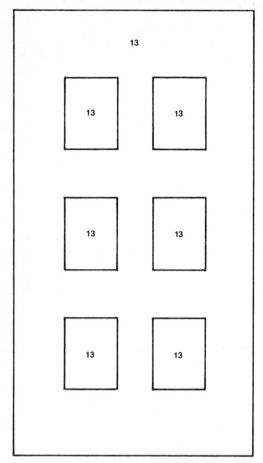

Make 1 for front

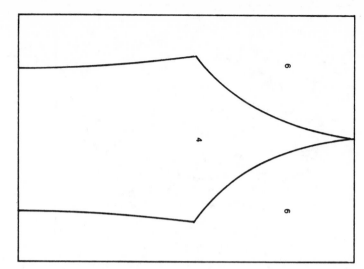

Make 3 for lower back

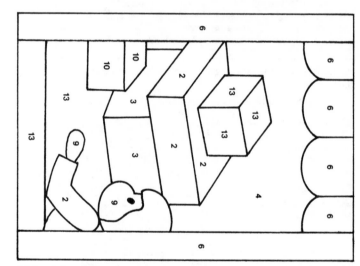

Make 1 for front

Make 2 for porch railing

Flow-in Icing Key
1 Lavender
2 Red
3 Green
4 Gold
5 Light blue
6 Dark blue
7 Light brown
8 Dark brown
9 Flesh
10 Orange
11 Black
12 Black with blue
13 White

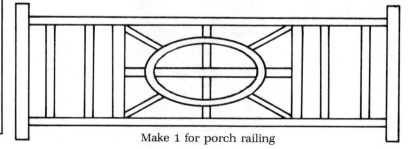

Make 1 for porch railing

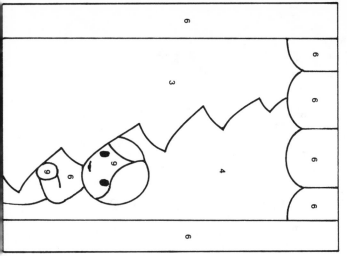

Make 1 for front

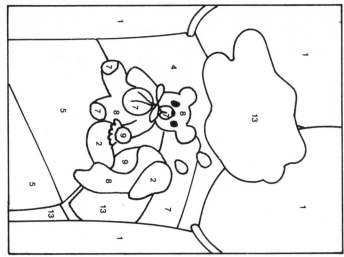

Make 1 for front

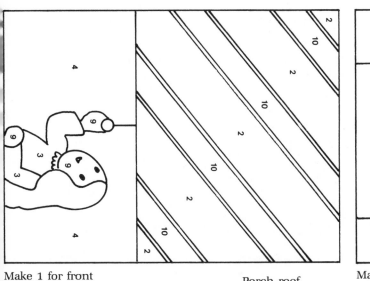

Make 1 for front

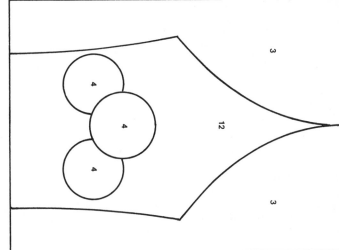

Make 2 for upper back

Porch roof
and
porch floor

2"

4⅜"

Roof

1¼"

14"

½"

5½"

15"

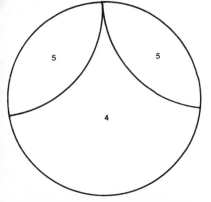

Make 1 each for front and back

Pattern pieces continued from page 145

Contributors

Design: Carol Middleton
Editorial Assistance: Shelley Ticheli Stewart, Linda Stewart
Cover Photograph: Charles Walton
Art: Carol Middleton, Steve Logan, Don Smith, David Morrison
Production: Jerry Higdon

Special thanks to the following people at *Southern Living* for their expert advice and time: Jean Wickstrom Liles, Susan Payne, and Bruce Roberts.

Designers

Lena Anderson, angels, soldiers & santas 70.
David B. Conard, reindeer 20.
Inez Crimmins, needlepoint sparklers 62.
Alexandra Eames, metallic foil fans 35, tree top angel 35, vine wreath 36, marbelized & painted eggs 36.
Carol Germek, herbs of Christmas 37.
Sara Gutierrez, angel pocket 61.
Jan Kirkpatrick, seashell wreath 26, Christmas lace 56.
Steve Logan, Christmas cardinals 46.
Denise May-Levenick, cross-stitched ornaments 60.
Ellen McCarn, gingerbread house 74.
Candy McMillan, memory tree 41.
Ken Neal, baker's ornaments 64.
Sunny O'Neil, good fortune chain 30, peanut garland 31, orange basket 31, cotton santa and lady 31, tree of ribbons 41.
Cynthia Parsons, smocked sherbets 63.
Susan Payne, gumdrop wreath 66, vegetable wreath 110.
Kaye Pendley, nature lover's tree 32, the pungence of pomanders 55.
Diana Perron, herb vinegars 112.
Rosalyn Smith, patchwork wreaths 65.
Tullie Smith House Restoration, goodie string 38.
Linda Stewart, ribbons & raffia 66, tiny tabletop tree 68.
Shelley Ticheli Stewart, the birds' gift 22, luminaries 25, fire starters 47.

Cameron Ticheli, ring around the candle 69.
Carol Tipton, partridges and pears 50, Christmas album 53, holly place mats 58, jolly St. Nick 59.
Gary Trentham, a Southern welcome 19.
Mark Vernon, scrolls & ribbons 43.

Photographers

© **Wilton Abel** 1982, top left and top right 12.
William A. Bake, top left 9.
Jim Bathie, 40, top left 41.
Mike Clemmer, top 10-11.
Dick Dietrich (photo appeared first in *Phoenix Home/Garden*), 7.
Carl V. Edington, Jr. for Milacron's *The Wonderful World Beneath The Christmas Tree*, top 4, top 5.
Otto Fenn, bottom 48.
Robert Flynn, 23.
Mary-Gray Hunter, 29, 38, 60, bottom 66.
Mac Jamieson, 64.
Louis Joyner, top right 8, 14, 15, 17.
Bob Lancaster, top 45.
Taylor Lewis, 89, 93.
Sylvia Martin, 20-21.
Beth Maynor, 18, 19, 22, 24, 25, 26, 30, 31, 32, 33, 37, 39, 42, 43, 44, 46, 47, top 48, 51, 52, 53, 54, 55, 56, 57, 58, 59, 65, 67, 68, 69, 70.
Judy A. Nemeth, 61.
John O'Hagan, top right 41, bottom 45, 62, 63, 72, 83, 110, 111.
Robert Perron, 112.
Bruce Roberts, 6, top left and left 10, bottom 11, bottom 12.
Jody Schwartz, top right and center and bottom 9.
Shelley Ticheli Stewart, top left 8.
Bill Strode (Black Star), bottom left 8.
Donald E. Thompson, bottom left and bottom right 4, center and bottom 5.
Charles Walton, cover, title, 1, 3, 13, 27, 34, 35, 36, 49, top 66, 71, 73, 75, 81, 84, 90, 94, 97, 105, 106, 107, 113, 114, 115, 116, 117, 118, 119, 120, 121, 122, 123.